A SAILOR'S

The life and times of John Short of Watchet
1839 – 1933

Tom Brown

Contents

Acknowledgements

My grateful thanks go to:

Market House Museum, Watchet, for permission to use the photographs of Watchet harbour and Thomas Chidgey's painting of *Annie Christian*. To the **National Library of Australia** for permission to reproduce the image of *Queen of the South*.

Mark Myers for access to the papers of his father-in-law, Michael Bouquet, which concern John Short, and also for Mark's contributions to the original shows and projects which led us to discover John Short. **Marilyn Tucker** of **Wren Music** for research, way beyond the call of duty, in crew agreements, log books, and other periodic returns from ships on which John Short sailed, which now reside in the Newfoundland University maritime archives.

Barbara Brown for encouragement, research assistance, patience and proof reading; **Jim Mageean** and **Jeff Warner** for sharing knowledge and debating issues; **Malcolm Taylor** formerly of the **Vaughan Williams Memorial Library** for help, knowledge, and permission to use archive material from the library; to **Jim Nicholas** (Watchet Market House Museum) and **Taffy Thomas** (the first storyteller laureate) for additional bits of information; to **Brian Richards** (Swansea vessels and mariners website) and **Mick O' Rourke** (Irish shipwrecks website), for confirmation relating to the collision of the *Crescent* and the *Queen of the South*. Thanks also go to the staff and volunteers who assisted us at record offices and maritime archives at London's Guildhall and in Taunton, Bristol, Falmouth, Newcastle, & Liverpool.

Chris Roche for knowledge and experience – both of shanties and because he's one of the few people who've actually done the job and sailed a square-rigger round Cape Horn! Particularly to **Chris Roche and The Shanty Crew** for generous support for the Short Sharp Shanties project.

I am also indebted to those who had conducted original research into John Short before us - to Dave Bland in local newspapers; to Watchet historians Ben Norman and Michael Bouquet; to journalists like Peter Hesp and Jack Hurley, and to custodians and recorders of tradition like the Market House and Boat Museum activists in Watchet. A full list of sources is included in the bibliography.

Introduction

I first became aware of John Short in 1979. My wife Barbara and I were creating two shows to be staged at The Lobster Pot restaurant and bar in Instow, in celebration of the maritime history of North Devon and the surrounding area, and as fundraisers for the then newly-formed North Devon Maritime Museum at Appledore on the Torridge estuary. In Cecil Sharp's manuscripts we found the material that he had collected from John Short in Watchet in 1914 and included some of his shanties, both in the shows and in the subsequent fundraising cassette *Over The Bar*.

JOHN SHORT. photo by Cecil Sharp, 1914 © EFDSS

Ever since that initial encounter with John Short, we had wanted to record the whole of his repertoire: his relatively early versions of the deep-water working songs that he had gleaned and used around the world in the second half of the 19th Century. That task is now complete, with an international crew of singers and musicians, a series of three CDs, and detailed documentation on the internet about

4

John Short's versions and how each came to be arranged and recorded. In undertaking that project, John Short – or 'Yankee Jack' as he was locally nicknamed – became very real to me and I felt the need to explore his life story: to discover who he was and to investigate the history through which he lived, the ships he sailed on, and where he went - all as part of understanding the man, his world, and the shanties he sang. What was found vividly illuminates not only John Short's world and his shanties but many of the other songs and narrative ballads that passed into the wider oral tradition – and from many of which I find myself quoting verses in this book.

It is rare to be able to detail a working man's life in this way and it is only possible in John's case because he was a local hero, and because of legislation requiring detailed record-keeping in the merchant marine 'lest the wars should rise again.' As with local heroes everywhere, Yankee Jack's story has accreted its own mythology of tales, anecdotes and elaborations - what academics call the *metafolklore* which surrounds the core facts. Some, on closer examination, have proved to be no more than a sailor's yarn – but good storytelling nevertheless. I have sought to address the discovered inaccuracies in John's reported story, as well as fill the gaps in his actual history.

John Short proudly kept the discharge papers from several of the ships on which he sailed (although from none of his earliest), and from these it has been possible to pinpoint several of his voyages. The papers themselves now appear to be lost but local historian Michael Bouquet noted several dates of signing on and discharge from them when they were in the custody of John's son George. For a sailor in the mercantile marine, a good discharge was important – it was the difference between finding your next berth on a sound well-run ship or ending up on a hell-ship.

> *If you want a merchant ship to sail the seas at large,*
> *You won't have any trouble if you've got a good discharge*
> *Signed by the Board of Trade – and everything's exact*
> *There's nothing in a limejuice ship contrary to The Act.*
> (THE LIMEJUICE SHIP)

The particular Act of Parliament to which this song relates and which, consolidating earlier Merchant Shipping Acts on the way, regulated conditions in merchant ships, would not be introduced until much later in the nineteenth century - for now, the better your discharge, the better you could choose where you wanted to sail, on which ship, and with whom.

John Short was not a diarist nor, as far as we know, did he write many letters: there is no singular archive source for major insights into his life, only aggregations of sometimes tangential information from which his story can be constructed. From various sources, it is possible to put some of his other voyages in order, but there are some where only the name of the vessel, or perhaps a destination, are recorded from informal interviews with John which were subsequently published. As a result of this range of sources, the quality, type and detail of the information varies enormously. Several bits of information about John and his life appear more than once in published form – later writers tend to borrow from earlier ones (they also occasionally elaborate, or even present hyperbole as fact). The earliest references have been used when borrowing has evidently occurred, but this is not an academic discourse and so sources are listed in the bibliography rather than specifically cited on each occasion. There are certainly voyages for which, on the face of it, we have no solid evidence at all and there are similarly a number of gaps in the chronological detail of John's life.

John was a humble man, if exceptional in certain ways, and the history of humble people is not documented as they live their lives. The *Crew List* agreements, which would be the obvious source for some more detail, were dispersed by the British government in the 1970s and those that were not destroyed ended up in sampled fragments in a number of County Record Offices; British and Canadian maritime museums; the National Archive and other locations. Nevertheless, where relevant crew lists and log books have been tracked down, they have provided additional detailed information and references to both the voyages he made and the vessels that he sailed in – some, indeed, that are not quoted by any of his interviewers.

Lloyd's Register of Shipping, the *Mercantile Navy List,* and *Lloyd's List* have all provided additional detail in the search for John Short's ships and voyages but, as will be shown, there are still gaps we cannot with certainty now fill. *Lloyd's Register* (LR) lists vessels registered at insurance agents Lloyd's of London and which were in excess of a hundred tons with origin, port of registry, dimensions, names of the managing owner(s), the master, tonnage, voyage destination, work done on her and a Lloyd's rating. It does however occasionally prove inaccurate or misleading.

The *Mercantile Navy List* (MNL) lists British registered vessels over a quarter of a ton. It lists only the vessel's name, port of registry, signal code and tonnage but does include the ship's official number which, rather like the chassis number on a car, is unique to the ship irrespective of any change of name and is never re-used for another vessel. However, the MNL too is not always abreast of the times. Both the LR and the MNL contain a variety of additional information which is not pertinent to this study.

Lloyd's List was, and indeed still is, a newspaper recording ship movements, arrivals, sailings and other incidents from all around the world. Fortunately, there is also an *Index to Lloyd's List* which, for the period we are considering, is indexed on a yearly basis. All the references to any particular vessel, citing the vessel's Master (not her official number) to distinguish between those of the same name, are listed together. By taking entries from the *Index*, checking the references in the *List* itself and then consolidating the entries again, it is possible to reach a detailed, if sometimes fragmentary, record of individual voyages. This method has been used extensively to try and determine the sequence of ships and voyages on which John Short sailed when there are no exact dates from his discharge papers, nor appearances in ship's logs.

Out of all this - this book is the result. I had originally intended that it should contain just John's life history and that of the ships on which he sailed. Although it was not part of the original intention, I have been persuaded to include John's shanties as well. Where John's texts were brief, they have been extended with typical verses from other versions. I hope this volume now covers all aspects of this exceptional man.

I want to thank profoundly the people who have financially assisted the overall project – not with a view to a return but because they, like we, believed it was worthwhile and that John Short was worth celebrating.

Tom Brown
Combe Martin
July 2014

A SAILOR'S LIFE

THE LIFE AND TIMES OF
JOHN SHORT OF WATCHET
1839 – 1933

John Short - also known locally by his nickname of 'Yankee Jack' - was a British merchant seaman from the days of sail. He started working coastal cargo boats in his youth, up and down and across the Bristol Channel near Watchet in the County of Somerset, England, where he was born, and went on to be a deep water sailor. His voyages took him all over the world: from Quebec to Mobile Bay, round Cape Horn and up to Callao: to India, China and Japan and down to Australia. He would be paid off from one ship at the end of her voyage and, when he felt the time was right or the money ran out, would seek to find another berth - working from trip to trip. In time, John retired from the deep water trade and returned to his place of birth where he continued working on vessels in the home trade and then acting as a 'hobbler', a sort of harbour towing pilot, well into his eighties. He was a happily married man. He and his wife were survived by a son, George. He enjoyed singing. He died in 1933, in his 95th year, and was buried in the local churchyard.

On the face of it, this life was not remarkable. It followed a pattern familiar to thousands of other men from coastal ports around the British Isles during the huge expansion of shipping and trade which followed the American War of 1812 and which, under canvas, continued through to the coming of the supremacy of steam.

What initially makes John Short special is that, when he was visited by the great English folk-song collector Cecil Sharp in 1914, Sharp collected fifty-seven songs from him, all but one of them deep-sea shanties. John Short was not merely a sailor who happened to remember a few shanties – he had been a shantyman: someone who was taken on the crew because, in addition to being an experienced seaman, he had the ability to lead work songs that kept a crew working at hauling or heaving in a concerted and efficient way: songs with texts that told a ribald tale, gave a commentary on the work in hand, or parodied a current popular song, but always reflecting the sailors' experience or stimulating their interest. As Richard Runciman Terry puts it in *The Shanty Book*: 'A good shantyman with a pretty wit was worth his weight in gold.' One good shantyman, it was said, was as good as five extra men on the rope or round the capstan: such a one was John Short. Tony James, a local journalist and deeply involved in Watchet's maritime history, says of him that 'He took his job seriously, once remarking that sailors co-ordinated by the right shanty could often do a job in half the time.' It is also apparent that John's voice and his command of singing were exceptional: even Cecil Sharp observed that 'His voice is rich, resonant and powerful, yet so flexible that he can execute trills, turns and graces with a delicacy and finish that would excite the envy of many a professional artist.' His voice was also loud and, according to Peter Hesp, when John was town crier for Watchet after his retirement from sailing, he could be heard two miles away from Watchet in Doniford.

Because of the time at which John was sailing on deep-sea vessels, his versions of these work-songs were relatively early in the development of shantying which, in the form in which it is now generally understood, really started in the first half of the 19th century after the 1812 Anglo-American War. The heyday of shanty creation was, however, short-lived and authorities on the subject, like Stan Hugill, were able to claim that 'it can safely be said that from 1860 onwards the production of new shanties ceased completely.' 'Certainly', said Doeflinger, 'most seem to have originated between about 1820 and 1860.' Other authorities concur. Short's versions therefore are early – certainly compared to the versions familiar to later collectors and authors like Stan Hugill, who was starting to acquire his repertoire some six decades after John Short started his deep-water career. Looking at the repertoires, one now sees that some shanties had changed over time, some had all but disappeared, and others had remain almost unaltered from the earliest record.

When he died, in 1933, Yankee Jack's passing was noted with an obituary in *The Times* – he was the most famous shantyman in England. He had lived through times of huge change – an ordinary man working his way through life. It was a life shaped by wars; the ascendancy of iron and steam; the development and growth of international trade; the tribulations of Empire and the emancipation of slaves; by commodity markets, industrialisation and emigration. He had learnt and sung his shanties around the world as the ships on which he served took soldiers to the Crimea, emigrants to Australia, tea from China, sugar from Mauritius, timber from Quebec and copper from Callao. Even so, John spent more of his sailing life in coastal vessels than he did in deep-sea ships

But let's begin at the beginning!

1839 March

> *As I was a-walking down Watchet's Swain Street*
> *A jolly old shipmate I chanced for to meet*
> *Hello, brother sailor, you're welcome to home*
> *In season to Watchet, I think you are come.*
> (THE WATCHET SAILOR)

In a small cottage at the head of Swain Street, Watchet, Somerset, just a few yards from the harbour, John Short was born on 5th March 1839. His father Richard, who had been born in 1816, was skipper of a small coastal schooner, the *Friends* of Watchet. He was married to Mary (née Boone), born at Stogumber in the same year as himself. John was christened at the parish church, St. Decuman's, on 21st April. He was the firstborn of the family, and he was to be followed by five sisters (Ellen, Louisa, Sarah Ann, Mary Jane and Clara) and two brothers (Sydney and Henry).

WATCHET HARBOUR –19TH C.   © Market House Museum, Watchet

Coastal trade around the British Isles was flourishing as it had done for centuries past for, until the coming of the turnpikes and the metalling of the roads, the shipping of supplies and commodities around the coast and up the estuaries and rivers was often quicker, easier and cheaper than trying to take it by road. Watchet, lying as it does on the southern shore of the Bristol Channel a little to the east of Minehead, was a not insignificant port, but in addition to the coastal and home trade in which John's father and many other local skippers were engaged, the 'Severn Sea' also saw the passage of deep-water vessels, the schooners and square-riggers, sailing up to Bristol, a port built on post-Elizabethan exploration and the slave trade, or to Gloucester Docks or the South Wales ports.

The Napoleonic Wars (1799-1815) and the Anglo-American War (1812-1815) were over and past, and worldwide trade had been booming, led by American-built ships of a sleeker style than the old 'wooden walls of England' that had made Nelson's Navy. The East India Company (EIC) – 'John Company' as it was familiarly known - formed and given a Royal Charter by Elizabeth I in 1600 - had, only five years before John Short was born, seen its monopoly of trade into China broken under:

> 'An Act for effecting an Arrangement with the East India Company, and for the better Government of His Majesty's Indian Territories, till the Thirtieth Day of April One thousand eight hundred and fifty-four. [28th August 1833.]'

Whereby,

> 'III. Provided always, and be it enacted, That from and after the Twenty-second Day of April One thousand eight hundred and thirty-four the exclusive Right of trading with the Dominions of the Emperor of China, and of trading in Tea, continued by the said Act of the Fifty-third Year of King George the Third, shall cease.'

John Company's monopoly and power in India had already been broken by the British government, due to the fact that the international company had become economically and politically more powerful than the government of the country that had given it birth. It was now closed down and forced to sell its assets - and that included its fleet.

> 'IV. And be it enacted, That the said Company shall, with all convenient Speed after the said twenty-second Day of April One thousand eight hundred and thirty-four, close their Commercial Business, and make sale of all their Merchandize, Stores, and Effects at Home and Abroad, distinguished in their Account Books as Commercial Assets, and all their Warehouses, Lands, Tenements Hereditaments, and Property whatsoever which may not be retained for the Purposes of the Government of the said Territories, and get in all Debts due to them on account of the Commercial Branch of their Affairs, and reduce their Commercial Establishments as the same shall become unnecessary, and discontinue and abstain from all Commercial Business which shall not be incident to the closing of their actual Concerns, and to the Conversion into Money of the Property herein-before directed to be sold, or which shall not be carried on for the Purposes of the said Government.'

John Short would one day be sailing on one of those old EIC ships. In that same year of 1833 the Canadian steamship *Royal William* took 25 days on the first east-west Atlantic crossing made entirely under steam, and five years later, in the year before John Short was born, Isambard Kingdom Brunel's *Great Western* set a new crossing record, beating sail for the first time. Despite this advent of successful steam boats, it would be another thirty-six years before the most famous of all the square-rigged tea clippers, the *Cutty Sark*, would be launched and she would continue to carry tea from China until 1877.

Emigration was also gathering pace, and the Western Ocean packet-ship lines were servicing the transatlantic trade. Packet ships, originally so-called as they carried packets of communications and post around the world, rapidly adapted to further trade opportunities. The Blackball Line, perhaps the most famous of all, had been the first company offering a scheduled regular service between Liverpool and New York. It had started back in 1817, sailing on the 1st and 16th of each month, whatever the weather. Emigration was boosted, not least by the Great Irish Famine of 1845-52 when almost a million of the Irish population sought escape from impoverishment and starvation in their native land. The Blackball Line developed a reputation for fast and tidy ships – but also for harsh discipline and vicious Officers.

> *In the Blackball Line I served me time*
> *To me way, ay, ay, hoorah, roll*
> *In the Blackball Line I wasted me prime*
> *Hoorah for the Blackball Line*
>
> *A bully mate and captain too*
> *To me way, ay, ay, hoorah, roll*
> *They're the bastards for to push her through*
> *Hoorah for the Blackball Line*
> (THE BLACKBALL LINE)

The California gold rush of 1849 was still to come; the Crimean War (October 1853 ~ February 1856) and the American Civil War (April 1861 ~ April 1865) were still to come. Through all of these, and more, John Short would be sailing.

1848 – 1856

John first went to sea, on an occasional basis in 1848, when he was only nine years of age, helping his father Richard in the coastal trade. The 1851 census finds him living with his parents in Swain Street, together with five younger siblings. From 1852, the year she was built, Richard Short was skipper of *Friends* of

Watchet, and he remained master of her for many years to come, as will become evident. At fourteen years of age, John joined his father full-time taking coal, timber and lime in and out of the Welsh ports. But the coastal trade was not for the young John Short: he wanted adventure.

> *A sailor's life is a merry life*
> *They rob young girls of their heart's delight*
> *Leaving them behind to weep and moan*
> *They never know when they will return*
>   (A SAILOR'S LIFE)

He had seen the tall ships sailing up and down the Bristol Channel: he had met the seamen who sailed them in Barry, Swansea or Cardiff or even in Watchet itself, where the 'hobblers' met the big ships, helped with the sails and then attached ropes and towed them into the harbour with rowing boats. John decided to go deep-sea.

The actual dates of his first voyage overseas are not certain. Reportedly, when he was eighteen, John together with two other young men of Watchet, William Smith and Edwin Chidgey, each a couple of years older than himself, signed on board the barque *Promise,* of London. Their voyage was to Cadiz and thence across the Western Ocean (Atlantic) to Quebec. Although his schooling had been minimal, John could read and write and sign his own name when many of his fellow sailors could only make their mark against where the Captain had written their name.

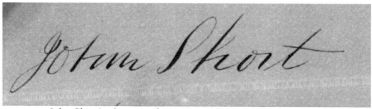

John Short's signature from a crew discharge of *Conference*

This triangular trade, between ports in the West Country, Canada and the Atlantic seaboard ports of Southern Europe had begun in the 17th Century, taking general wares from England to the Canadian plantations, salted wet and dry cod to Europe, and wine and brandy back to England. The trade developed over the ensuing two centuries – at times almost in reversal of the original pattern, by collecting salt at Cadiz which was shipped to Canada for preserving cod. The cod trade had started in the early 1600s and continued until the final collapse of the cod stocks some three and a half centuries later. Many Canadian ports started life as small colonies – plantations as they are known - around cod-processing stations and subsequently developed trade in furs and timber. By the 19th Century, the trade in timber had expanded hugely and ships from Canada would return laden, both in the hold and (in order to maximise cargo) on deck, with timber from the lumber camps. Such a one was the *Promise*.

On 27th March 1856 *Promise* sailed from Bridgwater in Somerset for Quebec, arriving home in mid-December. In February 1857 she sailed from Cardiff for Cadiz and thence to Quebec, arriving back to London in August. Her next voyage was from London to Quebec and back, from August 1857 to Christmas Eve of that year. John was not eighteen until 5th March 1857, but given the specific inclusion of Cadiz in his reported voyage, and the fact that *Promise* had sailed there from a local port, it seems most likely that it was the February to August 1857 voyage on which the three lads from Watchet sailed.

> *Was you ever in Quebec?*
> *Stowing timber on the deck*
> *Where you break your bloody neck*
> *Riding on a donkey*
>
> *Way, hay, and away we go*
> *Donkey riding, donkey riding*
> *Way hay, and away we go*
> *Riding on a donkey*
> (DONKEY RIDING)

The donkey referred to in this shanty, and in many others, is not the beast of burden but a 'donkey engine', a mechanical hoist system, latterly often steam powered, which was widely used in the logging, mining and maritime industries in the 1800s. On board ship it was mostly used alongside the quay for loading and unloading cargoes.

Promise's voyage took some five months from 4th February 1857: she is recorded off Gravesend on her return journey on 10th August 1857. It was on this trip, John told the Watchet historian Michael Bouquet, that he learnt his first two shanties, *Cheer'ly Man* and *Stormalong*. He told Cecil Sharp that *Cheer'ly Man* was 'one of the first shanties ever invented and the one I learned first.'

Oh, 'Auley Aye Oh,
Cheer'ly man
Walk him up Oh,
Cheer'ly man
'Auley Aye Oh, 'Auley Aye Oh,
Cheer'ly man
(CHEER'LY MAN)

'Stormalong', or 'Stormy', who appears as a named character in many shanties, was never a real person – he was a concept (possibly with his name 'borrowed' in the first instance from a minstrel stage song); an exemplary shellback; the epitome of an old sailor of the days of sail and, betimes, a highly emotional reference point for an Old Salt.

Old Stormey he is dead and gone
To my way-ay Stormalong John
All from Cape Horn where he was born
A-ha, come along, get along
Stormy along John

Old Stormey's gone, I saw him die
And more than rain it dimmed my eye

I wished I was old Stormy's son
I'd have a ship of a thousand ton
(STORMALONG)

After that first voyage, the three young sailors from Watchet went their separate diverse ways, although we do know that Edwin Chidgey eventually retired to Padstow in North Cornwall from whence he used to pilot boats up and down the River Camel from Padstow to Wadebridge and where the family is still remembered. Sharp wrote in his notebook: 'He wished I could have met his old mate Chidgey.'

1857

There is now a gap in the record of John's voyages, from August 1857 (when *Promise* returned to London) to his identified voyage on *Hugh Block* starting in October 1858. This is certainly when he sailed on the *Cezimpra* of Bristol. She is sometimes wrongly cited as *Zecimpra* or even, in one case, as *Zeumpia*. On her, John sailed to Catania, on Sicily, and to Malta. Registered at Bristol from 1856, the *Cezimpra* sailed regularly, primarily from Cardiff, into the Mediterranean. In the period between August 1857 and October 1858 she undertook three trips:

August or September – 22nd November 1857
22nd December 1857 – 5th May 1858
12th June – 2nd September 1858

Arriving home on the *Promise* on 10th August 1857, John could easily have travelled from London to Cardiff to sail on the first of these three trips (the actual sailing day from Cardiff is unknown – only that the *Cezimpra* departed Denia, in Alicante, Spain, to return to London on the 16th October). He could also have sailed on the second of the voyages. The third voyage, from June to September 1858, was to the island of Nevis in the Caribbean - not the Mediterranean - and can therefore be discounted. On balance, given that John rarely left a great deal of time between voyages at this stage of his career, it is probable that it was the first of the two voyages on which he sailed. This would also result in a period between the *Cezimpra* and his next certain voyage, on the *Hugh Block*, which will be returned to later in the story.

Cezimpra was fetching copper ore (one source quotes silver ore, but the ores would most likely be mixed metal in any case, copper, silver and lead ores frequently being found in association). The copper trade became more and more important to the shipping industry as the 19th Century progressed, and some insurers looked to 'copper bottom' ships to lower their risks. Sheathing, in felt and metal, is ubiquitous in the *Lloyd's Registers* of the 19th Century. Fouling of a vessel's hull would slow her down and reduce profitability, and shipworms could eat a boat to destruction. The main shipworm, Teredo worms, are not worms at all but bi-valve molluscs, a type of clam (*Eulamelli branchiata*) that bores into the underwater wooden structure of piers, wharves and the hulls of boats, and destroys them. The theory was that sheathing the hulls of ships with copper produced a poisonous film that deterred marine creatures. Copper sheathing was first suggested against fouling in 1708 but experiments, initiated in the Royal Navy, were not made until the late 1750s. Copper did well in protecting the hull from shipworms and other animals and in preventing the growth of marine weed.

Swansea already had a flourishing copper trade. It had been born and developed in the early 1700s and demand rose rapidly with the East India Company as a main customer, buying copper for the South Asia trade. Domestic use of copper also increased hugely in the 1700s and so Swansea was well placed to pick up the new demand from the Navy and Merchant Marine. Copper, however, was expensive.

In 1832, George Fredrick Muntz, a Birmingham metal-roller patented a 60:40 brass which became known as Muntz Metal or Yellow Metal. Production started at his mill in Birmingham, but demand outgrew the premises, and so a partnership was created with Pascoe Grenfell & Sons who produced it at their Swansea mill as 'Muntz's Patent Metal Company'. They fixed the price of the alloy at £18 per ton – 33% lower than the market price for the equivalent copper. Yellow Metal, laid over pitched felt became, almost instantaneously, the marine sheathing of choice. By 1843 the company was producing in the order of 4000 tons of yellow metal a year and demand would only grow. No wonder, then, that Swansea figured so prominently in the copper trade.

Yellow metal remained in constant demand because it sacrificed itself: sea water gradually dissolved it away taking any fouling with it. The records show that, on average, re-cladding was needed every three to five years. Copper and copper ore came from everywhere around the world: from some of the Mediterranean islands, where the *Cezimpra* sailed, to the West-coast ports of South America where John Short would soon be sailing.

October 1858 – August 1859

Another of John's reportedly early voyages was on the *Hugh Block*. She ran frequently to the West coast of South America, although her destinations were variable. John had said that, in the *Hugh Block*, he had sailed to Valparaiso and Iquique, and one particular voyage, with dates recorded in *Lloyd's List*, identify John's voyage precisely. *Hugh Block* left Liverpool on 29th October 1858 sailing down South around Cape Horn. Rounding Cape Horn could be a dangerous business, and one can do no better than quote an article about John Short from the *West Somerset Free Press* of August 1931:

> 'It took no less than six weeks to weather Cape Horn [in the *Hugh
> Block*], an experience by no means uncommon in the days of sailing
> craft. The "old man", the customary term for a captain, was not to
> be beaten so long as he could possibly carry on. Amid a succession
> of tempests, during which hot food was often out of the question
> and the crew lived and caught snatches of sleep in their saturated
> clothes, he fought his way round the dreaded headland, and no more
> delightful sight ever greeted the worn-out men than when the
> Chilean coast loomed up on the horizon.'

While beating up Magellan Straights it blew exceeding hard
While shortening sail, two jolly tars fell from the tops'l spar
By angry seas the ropes we threw from their poor hands were torn
We were forced to leave them to the sharks that prowl around Cape Horn

But when we got round the Horn, my boys, we had some glorious days
And very soon our killick dropped in Valparaiso bay
Those pretty girls came down in flocks – I solemnly declare
They are far beyond those Plymouth girls, with their long and curly hair
(THE GALLANT FRIGATE AMPHITRITE)

'Killick' is sailor-talk for the anchor. The cargo that *Hugh Block* carried back was, once again, copper ore. The West coast South American ports – the ports that were 'round the corner' of Cape Horn such as Valparaiso, Pisco, Callao, Ylo (pronounced 'high-low') and Iquique (pronounced 'I-kee-kee') - were long famous for the nitrate and guano trades: the mainland ports were also a significant part of the copper trade.

These Chilean and Peruvian ports were also some of the least developed and wildest according to Stan Hugill in his book *Sailortown*. Many a sailor, it was said, left his conscience nailed to the mast when he went 'round the corner', visiting brothels and grog-dens in his ports of call with impunity only to collect his conscience again when he doubled The Horn on the way back home.

O round the corner we will go
Around the corner Sally
To Callao through ice and snow
Around the corner Sally

I wish I was in Madam Gashee's
It's there I'd sit and take my ease

Was you ever in Valip'o
Where the girls put on a show

Was you ever in Ylo town
Where the girls will all go down
(ROUND THE CORNER SALLY)

Madam Gashee was the owner of a Callao brothel: her fame spread far and wide and she features in many a shanty. Callao was perhaps the most sophisticated of these relatively primitive ports in servicing Sailor Jack and possibly the most cosmopolitan of all the West coast South American ports. Ships from all nations and all trades up and down the West coast of the Americas took time out to visit, and John Short would be visiting Callao on more than one occasion, as we shall see. One individual Callao prostitute was even commemorated in her own shanty:-

In Callao there lives a whore,
Her name is Serafina,
        Serafina! Serafina!
She works all night and she sleeps all day,
In the old Calle Marina.
        Serafina! Oh, Serafina!

At screwing silly sailor boys,
No girl was ever keener
She'll make you pay right through the nose,
That lovely Serafina.

Serafina's got no drawers,
I've been ashore an' seen 'er,
She's got no time to put 'em on,
That hard-worked Serafina.
                        (SERAFINA)

Hugh Block arrived at Valparaiso on 10th March. From Valparaiso she sailed North to Iquique and, leaving there on 19th April, she made the London River on 28th August 1859.

September 1859 – September 1860

After his voyage around the Horn on *Hugh Block*, John's next voyage seems to have been on *Earl Balcarres*. Originally built in 1811 for the Honourable East India Company, she was an old type of East Indiaman and had become one of the best known ships of her day. Sold by the EIC in 1833 - as required under the Act cited above – she was bought by the Somes Brothers (who now owned many of the old EIC ships) in 1848. She still sailed to India, mainly commissioned by the British Government as a troop carrier.

We turn again to the *West Somerset Free Press*:

'In the early sixties, troops were taken to and from the various
stations overseas by sailing craft, often a most wretched voyage,
particularly for the wives and children of the men who accompanied
them. In the *Earl Balcarres,* Short made a trip to Bombay, whence
she proceeded to Karachi, on the Persian Gulf, and subsequently
returned to England. On the outward passage there were two deaths,
one of them being a soldier, but on the homeward trip no less than
four Service men succumbed. The ship's complement of crew and

19

passengers was, however, augmented by the number of births at sea.'

Once again, *Lloyd's List* provides details of the voyage this must have been: leaving London sometime in September 1859, *Earl Balcarres* sailed first to Cochin (now called Kochi) on the Southern West coast of India before sailing up to Bombay (Mumbai), where she arrived on 7th March 1860, and thence to Kurachee (Karachi). From here, *Earl Balcarres* sailed for London, the whole trip taking in the order of a year - for John's next embarkation was on 6th October. Short's trip was one of the last long voyages that *Earl Balcarres* ever made: on her next voyage she arrived at Bombay in a 'very leaky' condition, although she continued the India run until May 1863. Thereafter, no longer capable of such voyages, she was sold to the African Steam Ship Company for use as a hulk off the West coast of Africa.

EARL BALCARRES

October 1860 - January 1862

Having doubled both Cape Horn and the Cape of Good Hope, John's next voyage would take him even further afield – to China and Japan. In 1861 he sailed there on the *George Washington*. Although larger and larger ships were built from the 1830s onwards to maximise cargo on these longer trade routes, speed was also a consideration, and from the 1840s to the 1860s the 'extreme clippers' came to dominate the trade to Asia. Even so, smaller vessels could still turn a profit from lucrative cargoes: the Aberdeen-built clipper *George Washington* was a mere 414 tons.

Lloyd's List reveals details of the voyage: she sailed from London on 5th of October 1860, outward bound for Shanghai. She made two excursions from and back to Shanghai, to Swatlow and to Hong Kong, before sailing on to Kanagawa on the Southern Japanese island of Honshu where she loaded for London. Kanagawa was the place at which, only eight years before, Commodore Matthew Perry of the U.S. Navy had, following a show of force, imposed the *Convention of Kanagawa* which ended some two hundred years of isolationism and opened Japan to American markets and trade. It would also lead to the end of Japanese feudalism and the Shogunate. Subsequent Japanese treaties with the UK (1854), Russia (1855), France and the Netherlands (1858) were followed by a boom in trade with Japan. *George Washington* arrived back at London after a fifteen-month voyage on 15th January 1862.

> *'Twas a Yankee mate and a lime-juice skipper*
> *Blow, boys, blow*
> *They make her fly like a China clipper*
> *Blow me bully boys, blow*
>
> *Blow, boys, and blow for ever*
> *Blow, boys, blow*
> *And blow me back to the London river*
> *Blow me bully boys, blow*
> (BLOW, BOYS, BLOW)

It is not known what the *George Washington's* cargo was: she sailed from London within a month of the end of what became known as the Second Opium War, when China had effectively accepted that the opium trade was inevitable and instead chose to regulate it. The problem for the Americans and Europeans was that opium was just about the only thing that Chinese merchants wanted from those nations who were so eager to buy their tea, spices, textiles, and ceramics. Given her size, and the fact that the *George Washington* went directly from London to Shanghai and then voyaged (presumably trading) around the area, before finally loading in Japan to return home, it is probable that she was trading in textiles, ceramics or spices rather than tea.

Many sailors chose to spend their time on the Far East runs, rather than with bully mates on the Western Ocean packets with all the weather that the Atlantic could throw at them. These 'flying-fish sailors' would often take their ease ashore for an indeterminate time - 'on the beach', as Stan Hugill puts it - before taking another berth back home.

> As I was walking down Paradise Street,
>   Way ay knock a man down
> A Liverpool watchman I happened to meet
>   Give me some time to knock a man down.
>
> Says he, 'You're a Black Baller by the cut of your hair
> I know you're a Black Baller by the clothes that you wear.'
>
> 'O p'liceman, O p'liceman, you do me great wrong
> I'm a flying fish sailor just home from Hong Kong.'
>   (KNOCK A MAN DOWN)

Being away in the Far East, John does not appear in the April 1861 census – but his parents are still in Swain Street, now with seven children living at home.

Also, while he was on *George Washington*, the American Civil War had started. This proved to have a profound and long-lasting effect on maritime trade and a major boost to the development of maritime engineering. The first iron-clad war vessels appeared; the comparative manoeuvrability of steam vessels proved their worth; both sides rushed to develop and increase their navies, with Federal ships being built to blockade the Southern ports and the Confederate States building raiders to harry Federal shipping. Britain also benefitted, not only through the number of Northern ships which changed to British registry to evade the Southern raiders, but also in the number of ships that were commissioned and built in British ports. With the Americans becoming self-occupied, and other worldwide international trade being largely unaffected by the Civil War, increased opportunities for the development of commerce were handed to other maritime nations as competition decreased.

February - December 1862

After the *George Washington*, John Short next voyaged to Australia. This was in the ship-rigged 474 ton *Woodcote* and it is the earliest vessel for which there are exact dates from John's discharge papers. He signed onto the crew on 15th February 1862 and was discharged at Swansea nine months and twenty days later. Although penal transportation to Australia, introduced in 1787 (after the American War of Independence when Britain had lost the ability to transport convicts to America), was not finally abolished until 1868, it had become relatively rare even by 1857. However, the emigrant trade was now booming, not least because from 1847 (and until 1886) the British government offered, to approved persons, assisted passages to the new colony. Sometimes *Woodcote* took these emigrants, for she appears regularly in the records of emigration voyages from the mid-1850s and throughout the '60s, but always she carried general goods. Throughout her career, the records show that she sailed to Australia (usually Adelaide, but sometimes Hobart or Melbourne) via India (Rangoon, Calcutta, Madras) and Ceylon (now Sri Lanka).

Having been discharged at Swansea, on 5th December, it was only a short voyage across the Bristol Channel, in all probability catching a lift on a local boat, to spend Christmas and New Year at home in Watchet. All the indications are that John was not a drinking or hard-living man, indeed he is quoted as being a 'God-fearing man' and Cecil Sharp was later to note: 'He liked Padstow people because they were a quiet people (this means they were not public house men).' John Short did not fit the hell-raising image of the sailor on shore leave that some writers, and many of the surviving songs, have encouraged.

> *Come all you seamen bold who delight in a sailor's joy*
> *Come listen while I sing to you a song*
> *When Jack Tar he comes on shore with his gold and silver store*
> *There is no-one can get rid of it so soon*
>
> *The first thing Jack requires is good liquor to his hand*
> *Likewise the best vittals of every kind*
> *And a pretty girl likewise with two dark and rolling eyes*
> *Then Jacky Tar is suited to his mind.*
> (JACK ASHORE)

> *As I was a walking down Ratcliffe Highway*
> *A flash looking packet I chanced for to see*
> *I hailed her in English, she answered me clear*
> *I'm from the Blue Anchor bound for the Black Bear*
> *Sing too ra lye addie, sing too ra lye ay.*
>
> *She had up her colours, her masthead was low*
> *She was round in the counter and bluff in the bow*
> *She was bowling along with the wind blowing free*
> *She clewed up her courses and waited for me.*

I tipped up my flipper, I took her in tow
And yardarm to yardarm away we did go
She lowered her topsail, t'ga'n's'l and all
Let her lily-white hand on my reef-tackle fall.

In any case, society was moving on: by John's time, the frequency of sailors boozing and whoreing away their lump of pay from the voyage over a short period of time had reportedly declined massively.

Perhaps the situation was never as clear-cut as the songs of the time would pretend – many Sailor Jacks sought out their previous paramours and re-established a temporary bond: Henry Mayhew, in his illuminating 1862 study of the London poor, observed that:

> 'When sailors landed in the docks, and drew their wages, they picked up some women to whom they considered themselves married *pro tem,* and to whom they gave the money they had made by their last voyage. They live with the women until the money is gone (and the women generally treat the sailors honourably). They go to sea again, make some more, come home, and repeat the same thing over again. There are perhaps twelve or fifteen public-houses licensed for music in St. George's St. and Ratcliffe Highway: most of them a few years ago were thronged, now they can scarcely pay their expenses; and it is anticipated that that many of them will be obliged to close... The *fons et origo* of the declension is simply the institution of sailor's savings banks.'

January - August 1863

The Seaman's Saving Bank Act of 1856 offered an alternative to the constant cycle of earning, spending and having to go straight back to sea, and allowed for a more desirable future. Many merchant sailors (indeed, many more than the government had anticipated) took advantage of these new banks. There is no evidence as to whether John Short did or did not use one but it would be no surprise if he had done so. By the New Year, the wanderlust was back: no shellback could spend too long ashore and John was soon signing on for his next trip.

It was a voyage on which he was joined by the elder of his younger brothers, Sydney Richard. Sydney, now just 18, was doing as John had done, and what better way to undertake his first deep-sea voyage than under the watchful eye of his experienced older brother? John and Sydney would stay together for a couple of voyages to follow. The brothers signed on the *Benjamin Buck Greene* (widely known at the time as '*The BBG*') on the 4th January 1863, and the round trip to Mauritius lasted a little over seven months. John would make a second trip on the *Benjamin Buck Greene* three years later.

After the 1814 Treaty of Paris transferred the Isle de France (i.e. Mauritius) from French control to British, encouragement of sugar production on the island raised output to over 100,000 tons a year by 1854, and throughout the 1850s this one relatively small island was producing nearly 10% of the world's sugar. Poor soils were hugely enriched and made productive by the application of guano shipped in from the West coast and coastal islands of South America. Although sugar production would increase even further, Mauritius became less important in the trade overall as the Caribbean sugar plantations developed. The *Benjamin Buck Greene* made the trip to Mauritius for sugar, under a series of different masters and on an almost continuous basis, certainly from 1848 into the 1870s. She was owned throughout by H.D. & Jas. Blythe & Greene of Philpot Lane, London. The Blythe family were, together with the Barclays (of banking fame), also owners of three-quarters of the sugar estates on Mauritius.

The man himself, after whom the ship was named, was Benjamin Buck Greene (1808-1902), son of Benjamin Greene the brewer ('Greene King'). They too were deeply involved in the sugar trade, managing both their own and, on behalf of neighbours in Suffolk, other sugar plantations on St. Kitts in the Caribbean. Benjamin Buck Greene would become High Sheriff of Berkshire in 1865 and Governor of the Bank of England from 1873-1875.

The sugar trade was highly lucrative and closely guarded, but to maximise profits great care was needed with the cargo to ensure it did not deteriorate in the hold, and 'dunnage' was the key! Dunnage is defined as 'Anything placed between the skin of a ship and the cargo to prevent the latter from getting damaged.'

In his classic 1868 tome *All About Ships: the Life and Duties of a Sailor*, Cpt. Charles Chapman advises a Second Mate about his duties on 'the BBG' during a voyage to Mauritius and notes, of loading sugar, that:

> 'After the cargo is out, comes the time for laying the dunnage for
> sugar, and it will be as well to mention here again how careful you
> must always be with respect to dunnage. In Mauritius, small
> brushwood is often used, and should be continued right up the side
> to take off any leakage from the chain-plates, decks, or side. A
> continual dropping of salt water will ruin the whole of a bag of
> sugar, and that bag will perhaps destroy many others. Leakage not

only injures and wastes sugars, but makes them weigh heavier, which is of serious consequence in many ways.'

So, having sailed in the sugar trade to Mauritius, John and his brother were discharged in London in August 1863 – John on the 8th and Sydney on the 12th.

September 1863 - May 1864

There is then a month before both John and Sydney join *Queen of the South*. They had not moved far in the interim for it was still in London that they signed on. *Queen of the South* was an early steam-assisted sailing ship (the steam engine was an 300 h.p. auxiliary) fetching troops from the East Indies. Under the captaincy of William Stewart, she was on a voyage, as the log book cites, with 'Passengers and cargo from London for Cape of Good Hope, Madras, Calcutta and back to London.'

> *From the London docks we'll bid adieu*
> *To Sue and Kate and Kitty too.*
> *The anchor's weighed and the sails unfurled*
> *We're bound to cross the watery world*
> (OUTWARD BOUND)

QUEEN OF THE SOUTH (G F GREGORY) by permission of Nat. Library of Australia

The Short brothers signed articles on 15th September 1863. *Queen of the South* left the Victoria Docks on the 17th and anchored off Gravesend. Three seamen who had failed to board at the agreed time were each fined ten shillings when they did board (50p in modern currency, but over a week's wages at the time); two who had failed to arrive at all were declared deserters; replacements were signed on at Gravesend on the 21st and the ship sailed for South Africa. By 4th November she had dropped anchor in Table Bay off Cape Town and was unloading cargo. Apart from several seamen colluding in stealing a case of gin, and ending up 'drunk and incapable of doing their duty', the only episode of note was that one John Pattison, an Able Seaman (AB) who had been deployed as a 'trimmer', also became drunk and, for repeatedly refusing to do his duty, found himself locked in a spare cabin for five days until he relented. One can, perhaps, understand his frustration – trimming involved shovelling coal around in a hot, chokingly dust-laden, ill-lit coal bunker, to keep the load evenly spread and to feed coal to the firemen who stoked the boilers. Many an old sea-dog felt this was not appropriate work for an AB!

On 24th November *Queen of the South* was back at sea sailing for Calcutta, where she arrived in time for Christmas. She remained at the Calcutta moorings until 21st January. From there she sailed to Madras and then, about 6th February, sailed for home. There were a total of eighteen deaths on board during the homeward voyage. Apart from one child who died of convulsions, the remainder were all soldiers – two died of syphilis and two of dysentery, but the majority of consumption, i.e. tuberculosis. There were also four births at sea during the voyage.

There was little trouble with the crew on the return voyage but then, at 9:30 on the evening of 24th April off the Old Head of Kinsale, disaster struck. The logbook records:

'Captain Stewart being in charge of the deck. A lookout on each bow, 3rd Officer & Pilot looking out on the bridge, side & mast head lights burning brightly. Suddenly perceived the outline of a vessel about 3 lengths on the port bow in the act of putting out a green light before the main rigging. The vessel apparently standing on the tack being not more than 3 ships lengths off, bearing NE by N. The vessel was simultaneously seen by Cptn. Stewart, the lookouts, 3rd officer and Pilot.

'Cptn. Stewart immediately ordered the helm hard aport, reversed the engines full speed astern, at the same time letting the topsails run down - the 3 topsails being set at the time. All these orders being at once obeyed. Cptn. Stewart hoping that the vessel would also port his helm and throw all aback with his head to East. Had this been done the collision certainly would not have happened as the Queen of the South's head was fast going off to the Northward.

'However the vessel put his helm hard a starboard which caused his head to face off also to the Northward, at the same time making her way as the sails filled so fast that she struck the port bow of the Queen of the South with violence causing her masts to go by the board and apparently smashing in the whole of the starboard bow.

'As she appeared to be fast filling, the most urgent exertions to save the crew of the sinking vessel were made by the officers & men of the steam ship which was happily effected & minutes after the vessel sunk under the bow of the steamer. The vessel proved to be the Crescent of Swansea from Cadiz to Garston with a cargo of Copper ore.'

Crescent (official no. 4914) was a schooner of 147 tons, built in Plymouth, Devon, in 1818. She was registered at Liverpool in 1847 and subsequently transferred her registry to Swansea whence she worked in the copper ore trade until that fateful night when, apparently through her own neglect to mount adequate lights, she was in collision with a vessel some ten times her tonnage. The crew of the *Crescent*, all of whom had been rescued from the stricken vessel, were landed by the *Queen of the South* at Queenstown, Co. Cork (named Cobh prior to 1850 and after 1922).

Queen of the South continued to London and seven months and fifteen days after they sailed, on 4th May 1864, the Short brothers were discharged. John did not like steam ships: as the *West Somerset Free Press* article quoted above said:

'Like the average sailor of his day, Mr. Short detested "smoke stacks" – 'I wouldn't find 'em', he declared during the interview, and with sails and decks often begrimed with "smuts" the seaman's lot aboard them was by no means an enviable one. Going aloft amid a smother of smoke was certainly not a task to be envied.'

May - September 1864

On 9th May, five days after their discharge from the *Queen of the South*, the two brothers signed on board *Levant*. It was allegedly from this ship, possibly among others, that John would earn his soubriquet 'Yankee Jack'.

There is an often repeated story (the earliest source seeming to be Rouse's 1989 *Tales From Watchet*) that *Levant*, with John on board, was actually chased by the Confederate steam ship *(CSS) Alabama* during the American Civil War. Prior to Rouse's book, articles merely suggest that the *Levant* changed registry to Liverpool in order to avoid ships like the *Alabama*. *CSS Alabama* was a raider which had been built at Jonathan Laird's yard in Birkenhead on the river Mersey. She was commissioned in August 1862 and for nearly two years terrorised Northern Union shipping, boarding four hundred and fifty ships, seizing over two thousand prisoners and taking sixty-five Union vessels valued, at the time, at around $6 million.

Initially, in investigating this story, it became tempting to dismiss the tale of John being chased by *Alabama* and to put it down to a sailor's yarn. The Short brothers' voyage on *Levant* started on 9th May 1864 and was, according to *Lloyd's Register*, out to India.

The voyage finished at Liverpool on 10th September 1864 (four months & five days later), and the brothers were discharged on the 14th. The *Alabama's* voyage into the Indian Ocean, her sixth raiding expedition, was from September to November 1863 – well before the Shorts' voyage on the *Levant*. On 11th June 1864, the *Alabama* arrived at Cherbourg where her captain, Raphael Semmes, requested a dry dock in which to give his ship a much-needed overhaul.

So, in that one month overlap between the departure of *Levant* from London on 9th May, heading down to round the Cape of Good Hope on the way to India, and *Alabama's* arrival at Cherbourg on 11th June, having sailed round that same Cape en route from the Straights of Malacca to France, the two ships could have passed each other somewhere down the West coast of Africa, but that is all. In this scenario, *Levant* might have been sighted, but not chased or engaged, and there is no reference to *Levant* in *Alabama's* logs.

However, *Lloyd's List* contradicts *Lloyd's Register* when the latter states that this particular voyage of *Levant* was to India. It therefore became necessary to review and reassess the available information. It is apparent that the voyage destinations given in *Lloyd's Registers* are not infrequently incorrect. This may in part be due to the publication date necessitating an anticipation of destinations on the part of

29

the respondents but greater mistakes which occur (an example of which appears later), cannot be granted this excuse. *Lloyd's List,* which is invariably more accurate than the *Register* as it is contemporaneous with the actual events, details the voyage in question thus:

12/5/64	Gravesend – sailed for Boston
21/5/64	Deal – arrived from River, sailed for Boston
20/6/64	Boston – arrived from London
10/9/64	Liverpool – arrived from Boston

'River' or 'The River', which is frequently found in *Lloyd's List* reports, refers, with a presumption of which perhaps we should not be surprised, to The London River – The Thames – as if there were no other river of significance in the whole world!

The voyage from London to Boston and back takes *Levant* nowhere near India or the Indian Ocean, but simply forwards and backwards across the North Atlantic. From February to July 1864 *Alabama* was in the South Atlantic, raiding off the coast of Brazil and taking no less than 29 prizes and then, from August to September, she sailed off the coast of South Africa before venturing, as already noted, into the Indian Ocean. Even after reassessment then, it seems impossible that *Levant*, with John Short on board, was ever actually chased by the *CSS Alabama*.

Alabama was sunk off Cherbourg in June 1864 by the Union warship *Kearsarge.* Blockaded at Cherbourg, Capt. Semmes elected to bring his vessel out of port, beyond French territorial waters, and fight *Kearsarge.* The story of *Alabama* is itself celebrated in the shanty *Roll, Alabama, Roll* but it was not one that John Short was known to have sung.

> *Now a shot from the forward pivot that day*
> *Roll, Alabama, roll*
> *It blew the Alabama's stern away*
> *Oh, roll, Alabama, roll*
>
> *And off the three mile limit in sixty-four*
> *Roll, Alabama, roll*
> *The Alabama sank to the ocean floor*
> *Oh, roll, Alabama, roll*
> (ROLL ALABAMA ROLL)

Britain was theoretically neutral during the American Civil War and the British Government eventually had to pay compensation to the Union for the damage done by ships that had been built in England for the Confederacy – a total of some $15.5 million.

As can be seen in the history of *Levant* in Appendix 2, she had actually been a Liverpool-owned and registered ship for over four years before the start of the American Civil War, and crew lists show that she only had a couple of Americans in her crew – there were more Scandinavians! Thus, although the truth should never stand in the way of a good story, *Levant* had not, as reported in the *West Somerset Free Press* of 29th August 1931 (and subsequently quoted by several other writers), changed to British registry because of the conflict. Nevertheless, she is sometimes referred to as an 'American' ship and it is evident that Yankee Jack regarded her as American – indeed, this may be the origin of the frequent report that she *was* American. John liked the American merchant marine – largely, he told Cecil Sharp, because the food was better than on British ships.

In researching for this book, it became obvious that the term 'American', at that time, was applied with impunity to any ship from North America – including ships that we would now refer to as 'Canadian'. The 'Dominion of Canada' was only created in 1867, under the *British North America Act*, whereby New Brunswick, Nova Scotia, Quebec (Lower Canada) and Ontario (Upper Canada) were brought together. Prior to 1841, these two latter territories were known as the 'Province of Canada'. Other provinces were incorporated later but for any seaman sailing west across the Western Ocean, he was sailing to America - and any vessel with its home port on that side of the Atlantic was 'American'.

September 1864 – May 1866

John is believed to have sailed on the *Levant* more than once, and any additional voyage would, because of the chronology involved, have been after the voyage cited above and for which we have dates. The fact that he sailed on her more than once is also confirmed by the Crew Agreement from when he joined the *Benjamin Buck Greene* for his second trip, which shows that immediately prior to that, he had been on the *Levant*, from which he had been discharged on 9th May at Cardiff.

The whole of the twenty months, from September 1864 until May 1866, could have been spent on the *Levant* although consideration of the ships *Jane Gray* and *Mary Ann*, below, suggests otherwise. The record of *Levant's* voyages between September '64 and May '66 is fragmentary, but the most likely is the voyage that left Akyab (now called Sittwe – capital of the Burmese state of Rakhine), on the Bay of Bengal, in April 1866. She had sailed from England to Bombay (Mumbai) on unknown dates, left Bombay for Akyab on 21st December 1865, and left Akyab homeward bound on 22nd April. This could have just allowed the voyage to end in time for John to sign on his next ship on the 9th May.

Notwithstanding, all sources agree that it was from this voyage (or voyages) on 'American ships' that he earned his nickname of 'Yankee Jack', and it was undoubtedly at this time that the shanty *I Wish I Was With Nancy* – a shanty parody of Dan Emmett's *I Wish I Was In Dixie* – entered his repertoire.

The original had been written in 1859 and was widely popular, in both the Northern and Southern States, for a couple of years. In April 1861, after Louisiana had seceded from the Union, the theatrical troupe of Mrs. John Wood opened in John Brougham's burlesque *Powhatan and Pocahontas* at the New Orleans Varieties Theatre. At the first evening performance, as the last programme item, a number of elaborately dressed Zouave volunteers marched onstage, led by Mrs. Wood singing *I Wish I Was in Dixie*. The audience was ecstatic and demanded seven encores. Thereafter, *Dixie* became the war-anthem of the Confederacy.

> *ORIGINAL*
> *I wish I was in the land of cotton*
> *Old times there are not forgotten*
> *Look away! Look away!*
> *Look away! Dixie Land*
> *I wish I was in Dixie, Hooray! Hooray!*
> *In Dixie Land, I'll take my stand*
> *To live and die in Dixie*
> *Away, away, away down South in Dixie*
>   (I WISH I WAS IN DIXIE)

> *SHANTY*
> *I wish I was in the land of cotton*
> *Tickling up the old girl's bottom*
> *Down the strand, down the strand*
> *Down the strand, down the strand*
> *I wish I was with Nancy, I, O, I, O*
> *On the second floor, with two bob more*
> *I'd live and die with Nancy*
> *I, O, I, O, I'd live and die with Nancy*
>   (I WISH I WAS WITH NANCY)

'Two bob' was common parlance for two shillings in British pre-decimal currency – and a 'two-bob bit' was a coin known as a florin.

32

Parodies, and straight versions, of other Civil War songs such as *Maryland, Marching Through Georgia* and *John Brown's Body,* also passed rapidly into the repertoires of shantymen. Other shanties that Yankee Jack credited to his time on American ships were, according to Sharp's notebooks, *A Hundred Years on the Eastern Shore, Huckleberry Hunting, Liza Lee* and *The Sailor Likes his Bottle.* Although only these five shanties were explained to Cecil Sharp as being American in origin, the number of John's shanties which actually originate in American (mostly African-American) work-chants and vaudeville songs, and in less developed forms than later versions, give testimony to the huge number of shanties that originated in America, and may further explain why, given his repertoire, John's nickname became 'Yankee Jack'.

The African-American influence on the development of shanties in the 19th Century is difficult to overestimate. A great number of freed slaves went to sea: it was not easy to get a paid job where you'd once been a slave – nor would you particularly want to! As worldwide trade, particularly for North America, continued to expand, so did shipping, and labour was needed at sea. Many an African-American ended up on deep-sea ships, and it was the fusion of habitual rhythmic work-songs (from the slave field experience), vocal strength and narrative coming together from the Black American, the Irish, the English and other cultures that drove the development of shantying. And the seaman - black or white - was better paid than his landlubber contemporaries!

> *Oh a dollar a day is a hoosier's pay*
> *Lowlands, lowlands away*
> *A dollar and a half is a shellback's pay*
> *My dollar and a half a day.*
> (LOWLANDS)

By the time we locate Yankee Jack again, the American Civil War is well over, and trade is moving ever more freely around the world. Sydney Short seems to have gone his own way as he cannot be identified on any of John's ships after that first trip on *Tweed*. In fact, by mid-1868 at the latest, Sydney had returned to Watchet, for he married Elizabeth Ann Chidgey (b.1846) on 26th December 1868 and settled down. Sydney's experience was not wasted: he earned his Master's ticket and by 1869 he was skipper of *John* of Watchet, a 42-ton coasting vessel. According to the census of 1871, Sydney and Elizabeth were then living in Wine Street [*sic*], Watchet with their 1-year old daughter, Ada Annie. Another daughter, named Elizabeth Ann after her mother, was born on 15th July 1875 but tragically, by the time her birth was registered on 11th August, both mother and daughter had died.

May 1866 - January 1867

On 9th May 1866 – the same day as his discharge from *Levant* - we know, from both John's discharge papers and from the relevant crew-list documentation, that he embarked on his second trip on *Benjamin Buck Greene* to Mauritius. The trip took ten months and eight days, and he was discharged on 14th January 1867 in London. On both occasions *Benjamin Buck Greene* shipped out general goods, not least for the increasing population of Indian indentured labour which had eventually (and some time after the abolition of slavery in other British territories) replaced slaves on the island. Her homeward cargo was, again, raw sugar.

> *I wish I was in Mobile Bay,*
> *Rolling cotton all the day*
> *But I'm stowing sugar in the hold below,*
> *Below, below, below*
> (STOWING SUGAR IN THE HOLD)

The year of 1867 also saw the start of what would, in time, become a cause célèbre and a national movement to improve the lot of merchant seamen. It would lead to the parliamentary battles that Samuel Plimsoll waged over conditions, safety at sea and loading lines. In that year, the *Society for the Improvement of the Condition of Merchant Seamen* conducted a survey which was presented to the Board of Trade; it showed, amongst other things, that the average life expectancy of a merchant seaman was only forty-five years. Many died by the time they were forty, and generally they could expect their health to be 'broken down' by thirty-five. John Short, rather like his forefathers, would prove an exception to the rule: his father had died at eighty-four and his grandfather at ninety-two – John would live to be ninety-four.

April 1867 - September 1869

There is now a gap of three months ashore. During this time John evidently made his way from London to Cardiff – doubtless spending at least a little time at home in Watchet. It was from Cardiff that, on 25th April 1867, he sailed outward bound on the ship *Conference* of Bristol. She was a 966-ton square-rigged vessel built in 1856 at Richibucto, New Brunswick. The first destination for *Conference* on this trip was Callao - so once more John Short shipped around Cape Horn, but although going round the corner was this time without incident, *Conference* was not a happy ship nor was she to have a trouble-free voyage – as is revealed by the ship's crew list and log-book.

Her master, Emmanuel John Bolt of Appledore in North Devon, had been signing on crew in Cardiff since around 11th April and one seaman, John James of

Falmouth, died of fever before he even arrived for duty. By the 25th of the month the master had a full crew of twenty including the mate, 2nd mate, bosun, carpenter, sailmaker, steward and cook. The remaining thirteen members of the crew were each classed as 'AB' (able-bodied seamen), including John himself, now just turned 28, and two fellow Watchet sailors: John Wescombe, aged 19, second son of the local pharmacist and William Chidgey, aged 21, who, like John, had started working on local boats as a boy. There were also two sea apprentices in the crew.

Conference arrived at Callao on 22nd August – a five month trip all but three days – and shore leave was the order of the day. On 2nd September, when the crew were back on board and meant to be working, the log shows that at 6.30 a.m. four of the ABs refused to do so, claiming that they were 'in danger of their lives'. The two following days they continued to refuse and so at noon on the 4th, by order of the British Consul, two of them were jailed. The other two still refused to work as they were 'not happy with the ship' so, at 10.00 a.m. on the 7th, they were also jailed.

Once a sailor had signed Articles, he had formally entered a contract to sail with the ship. Subsequent refusal to sail with her, or even to undertake his duties on board, was a criminal offence for which he could be jailed. Although not pertinent in this case, it is salutary to realise that it was not uncommon for a sailor to prefer to be jailed rather than sail on what he regarded as a 'coffin-ship'. (The term 'coffin-ship' later came to be applied primarily to overcrowded emigrant ships, but it originated in often over-insured, badly maintained and over-loaded cargo vessels.) Samuel Plimsoll, in his 1873 polemic *Our Seamen: An Appeal*, which did so much to raise public consciousness about maritime safety and insurance fraud, cites several examples of sailors finding that the ship on which they had contracted to sail was so overloaded that they sought jail rather than risk almost certain death – and several of those examples also demonstrate that 'almost certain death' was not mere hyperbole!

> *I bought up an old rotten ship*
> *And filled it with boxes of earth,*
> *I swore they were boxes of Indian silk*
> *And insured them for ten times their worth.*
>
> *At sea, of course, she went down,*
> *Ten thousand I got for my greed;*
> *But Plimsoll is putting a stop to my game,*
> *And hang it, I think he'll succeed*
> (A COFFIN-SHIPOWNER'S LAMENT)

On the 14th September 1867, whilst a fifth AB from *Conference* was being taken to the Consul for refusal to work, he deserted. In fact, after the four previously jailed seamen returned to the ship, on the following morning, it was discovered they they too had all deserted. Thus, Her Majesty's Vice Consul at Callao signed *Conference's* log on the 1st October noting:

> 'Further that Charles Jackson, William Jones, Henry Stevens, Alfred Dowling and Peter Sinclair have been reported to me as deserters and a proper entry in the official log produced to me.
> British Consul, Callao, October 1 1867
> Douglas Hastings   H.M. V.Consul'

Meanwhile, on the morning of 10th September, the Mate, William Dibden, was sent to the hospital as he was 'sick'. Another AB also became sick and was hospitalised on the 16th. Then on 30th September, when the AB returned from hospital, the bosun William Keates managed to fall from the beams into the lower hold, break his right arm and receive 'a severe shaking': he too was hospitalised.

Thus, on 30th September, by which time *Conference* should have been back at sea and plying her trade, a quarter of her crew had deserted and the Mate and Bosun were hospitalised. Something had to be done. On 30th September and 1st October, five new crew members were signed on: previously on a variety of different ships, there were two British, one North American and two Spanish-speaking South Americans. The latters' English was, at best, limited, but the Vice-Consul signed that all had been done in the correct manner, and that he was satisfied that the South Americans understood the terms and duties of their engagement. The new crewmen were all taken on at a dollar rate of $90 per calendar month – the familiar dollar-and-a-half a day - but for a period limited to the forthcoming short voyage to get cargo. *Conference's* cargo was to be guano, and on 1st October she left Callao for Pisco and thence thirteen miles offshore to the Chincha Islands.

Guano is the general name for the accumulations of excrement from sea-birds, cave bats and seals which were excavated and used as fertiliser - for it was rich in both nitrogen and phosphate. The nitrate content was also used to provide one third of the composition of black gunpowder. The coast of Peru, particularly with its off-shore islands, produced many sites where guano had accumulated over centuries and was many tens if not hundreds of metres deep. From the 1840s, when Peru first started exporting it, demand for this wonder-fertiliser grew massively as a result of scientific evidence as to its properties. Peru's future economy seemed assured. Until the late 1860s, by which time the industry was in decline and sources running out, Peru enjoyed an economic boom known as the Guano Age.

Chinese indentured labour 'mining' guano on the Chincha Islands

The Peruvian Chincha Islands were such an important source of this highly commercial commodity that the former colonial power, Spain, which did not recognise Peru's independence, fought to regain the Islands in what became known as the Chincha Islands War. The Spanish occupation of the islands, which lasted from April 1864 until May 1866, was the initial stimulus for many South American countries to unite in a war that would finally repulse any re-colonising aspirations Spain may have had.

Conference arrived at the islands on 10th October 1867 – the year after the war ended – and, having loaded her cargo, departed on 9th December. The two months taken to achieve a full cargo is probably simply down to the huge number of ships that would have been waiting to load: reports from Iquique, another guano port, quote some two to three hundred ships in the bay at any one time!

Was you ever in I-kee-kee
Round and round the bloody bay
Loading bird-shit all the day
Riding on a donkey
(DONKEY RIDING)

Conference arrived back at Callao on 13th December and the five temporary crew members who had been signed on at the beginning of October were all discharged on arrival. Captain Bolt then set about signing up new crew members for the voyage home to replace the deserters and, as in the Far East sailortowns, there were always men 'on the beach' (who may well have been themselves deserters from earlier ships) ready for a short contract or a paid trip homewards with few questions asked. A Swede was signed on the 13th and five other ABs, including two Germans and a Belgian, on the 14th. The mate, William Dibden, also had to be replaced: he was still hospitalised and as a result was formally discharged from the crew as sick at Callao on 14th December and replaced by George Baker of Bristol. It must be assumed that the bosun, who had broken his arm falling into the hold three months previously and had consequently missed the excursion to Pisco and the Chincha Islands, was now fully recovered and able to resume his duties, for there is neither indication of a replacement for his rôle nor any amendment in the log. The crew was due back on board on the 16th but the Swede failed to turn up and so John Brown of Aberdeen was signed on in his stead. With a full crew, *Conference* left Callao, homeward bound, on 16th December 1867. The new crewmen had all been engaged at £4 12s 6d sterling (but with a dollar advance of $90). It is likely that this was a fixed fee for the voyage rather than a monthly salary for, as shown in *Conference's* next trip, an AB's salary was only £2 or £2 10s per calendar month.

Although the crew list and log-book give this wealth of detail, there are still many unanswered questions about the voyage. Why did a quarter of the crew refuse to work? Did they have genuine concerns about the ship? Did they anticipate problems with highly nitrogenous and potentially explosive cargo she was due to carry? Were they trouble-makers or were they just too content with the time they had had ashore, sampling the delights of Callao? Whatever the case, John Short completed the voyage with a V.G. (Very Good) rating for both his 'General Conduct' and his 'Ability in Seamanship' (although, to be fair, all the crew with the exception of the deserters had the same rating). He was discharged in Plymouth on 23rd April 1868 – a voyage of almost exactly one year.

Oh the times are hard and the wages low,
Leave her, Johnny, leave her,
It's time for us to roll and go,
And it's time for us to leave her.

Oh a stinking ship and a carping crew
For twelve long months we've pulled her through

We pumped her all around the Horn
It was pump, you bastards, pump or drown

Oh leave her Johnny, like a man,
Oh leave her Johnny while you can,
                    (LEAVE HER JOHNNY, LEAVE HER)

Whatever the experiences of that first trip on *Conference*, John sailed on her again three months later. In fact, he may have stayed with the ship as part of a skeleton crew taking her from Plymouth, where she had docked and unloaded, round to Cardiff ready for her next voyage, and in all likelihood, crossing over the Severn Sea to Watchet for a while. He had obviously done well on the previous trip – keeping his head down, even if not his voice as shantyman - and done his duty, because when he signed on again, at Cardiff on 28th July, he was taken on as Bosun. Evidently a sailor's rank did not affect his use on board as a shantyman – it was the skill and ability that counted, not the level of authority.

Although an AB shantyman might be excused all but light duties, he was not given extra pay! It is interesting to note the relative salaries (per calendar month) paid to the different specialists and crew on a ship of the time. *Conference's* paperwork for this voyage gives the following:

	Salary (p.c.m.) £.s.d	Advance £.s d	Allotment £.S.d
Master:	not specified		
Mate:	7/-/-	3/10/-	
2nd mate:	4/15/-	2/7/6	
Boatswain:	3/10/-	3/10/-	1/15/-
Carpenter:	3/10/-	3/10/-	2/15/-
Sailmaker:	4/10/-	3/10/-	2/10/-
Steward:	4/15/-	4/15/-	2/7/6
Cook:	3/10/-	3/10/-	
AB x10:	2/10/-	2/10/- –3/-/-	
AB x1:	2/-/-	3/-/-	

39

Prior to the introduction of decimal currency in Britain in February 1971, standard Sterling currency comprised Pounds (£), Shillings (s.) and Pence (d.). There were 12 pence in a shilling, and 20 shillings in a pound – and thus 240 pence in a pound. Cash amounts were written, as above, with a forward slash separating the pounds, shillings and pence, and a dash was used instead of a zero.

A sailor could make a monthly allotment, often of up to half or even two thirds of his pay, which could be drawn monthly by someone of his choice (most often a spouse or other dependant) ashore, pending his return. He could also take a month's advance on his pay to clear off debts ashore, renew his wet-weather gear, or whatever else was needed. The less careful sailor, drugged and 'shanghaied' away on a vessel not of his own choosing, could also find his advance had been taken by the crimp who shipped him away – with no benefit to himself or his kin.

> *With the best of intentions you never goes far*
> *After twenty-two days at the door of the bar*
> *I toshed back me liquor, and what do you think*
> *Some lousy old bastard had doctored me drink, and it's*
> *Roll, roll bullies, roll*
> *Them Liverpool Judies have got us in tow.*

> *The next I remember I awoke in the morn*
> *On a three skys'l yarder bound south round Cape Horn*
> *With one pair of oilskins and three pairs of socks*
> *And a jar of green ointment for curing the Pox*
> (ROLL, BULLIES, ROLL)

Thus, for the first month at sea, until his advance had been cleared, Sailor John was working for nothing. When the crew started earning for themselves again, they had an elaborate ceremony of 'The Dead Horse' – dragging an effigy of a horse around the deck, hoisting it up aloft, and dumping it in the sea. The most vivid and illuminating description of the custom (as well as of 'shanghai-ing') is to be found in Hiram Bailey's book *Shanghied Out of 'Frisco in the 'Nineties,* and I am grateful to Gavin Atkin of intheboatshed.net for introducing me to the book. The Dead Horse ceremony also had its own shanty:

> *For one whole month we rode him hard,*
> *And we say so, and we hope so,*
> *Now take him up to the highest yard,*
> *Oh, poor old horse.*

So now the month is up, ol' Turk,
Get up, old horse, and look for work.

Get up old moke and look for graft
While we lays on, an' yanks ye aft.

We'll hoist him up to the main yard high
And drop him down in the sea to lie.
                    (DEAD HORSE SHANTY)

John Short, according to the log, took his month's advance and was due to be on board on 1st August 1868 – the day she sailed. The Master, 2nd Mate, Steward and one AB (John's fellow Watchet sailor, William Chidgey) had also all been on the previous voyage – the rest of the crew were new to the ship and signed on at Cardiff. The *Conference* arrived at Caldera, in Chile, on the 15th November. The town lies within the area of the Atacama Desert and had become a major mineral exporting town since the first railway (from Copiapó) had opened at the end of 1851.

This time *Conference* was loading minerals – silver, copper and saltpetre (nitrate) are all widespread in the Atacama region and its hinterland: there is little else! She sailed again on 9th December, arriving at Callao on the 22nd, where one AB deserted. The trip was otherwise uneventful and the crew were discharged, after a thirteen months voyage, at Bristol, on 4th September.

As the Peruvian stocks of guano started to become exhausted, and prices rose in the late 1860s, many Western nations turned to Chilean mineral nitrates as the fertiliser of choice and there was open conflict between Peru and Chile in the 1870s, following this switch. John Short's first voyage on the *Conference* had been to the Peruvian Chincha Islands in 1867 for guano; his next trip, a year later and on the same vessel, was to the Chilean Atacama for a cargo of mineral nitrate. The two trips fell either side of this important cusp of change between the two provision and in the history of trade with South America.

1869 September

John had signed on the *Conference* as an AB in April 1867 and now, two and a half years later and after twice doubling Cape Horn, he was leaving her in September 1869 as bosun with, again, a 'V.G.' discharge.

The world was moving on, and for the merchant marine huge changes were in the offing. Transportation to Australia had formally ceased in 1868 but the new colonies were rapidly developing and seeking immigrants. The trade in which

41

John Short had sailed to Australia in 1862 on board the *Woodcote* was continuing to expand at a rate of knots. The Suez canal opened on 17th November 1869 after 10 years of construction. Suddenly, you could travel by water between Europe and Asia without having to go round Africa and the Cape of Good Hope. It instantaneously saved some 4000 miles and several weeks' sailing. Old habits, however, die hard and mistrust in the reliability of steam was widespread. 1869 also saw the building of and, on November 22nd, a mere five days after the opening of the Suez Canal, the launching of the *Cutty Sark*. The most famous of the tea clippers was effectively obsolete before she was even launched.

The issues and dangers of overloading and unsound ships were becoming a matter of public concern. If a passenger was lost at sea there was an enquiry – if it was a cargo boat, then a sailor's lost life was not worth the effort. It was not even obligatory for a cargo ship to be surveyed – in 1869 a bill requiring survey failed to pass in Parliament thanks to the power of the shipping lobby, although it did pass when re-presented a year later.

John had been sailing on deep-water vessels for some twelve years and had made Bosun. Steam was now in the ascendant and he must have looked to the future with reservations: he had his own opinion about what made a proper sailor – and steamships were not a part of it. His younger brother Sydney, with whom he had sailed the deep oceans, was back in Watchet, married, and the skipper of a coastal boat. All this must have played on John's mind.

Intermission

> *We've traded with the Yankees, Brazilians, and Chinese,*
> *We've laid with dusky beauties in the shade of tall palm trees.*
> *We've been through the Southern Ocean and up to Callao*
> *Around Cape Horn and back again, a sailor's bound to go.*
>
> *I've crossed the Line and Gulf Stream, been round by Table Bay*
> *Around Cape Horn and home again, for that's the sailor's way.*
>
> *In calm or storm, in rain or shine, the shellback doesn't mind.*
> *On the ocean swell, he'll work like hell for the girl he's left behind.*
> *He beats it north. He runs far south. He doesn't get much pay.*
> *He's always on the losing game for that's the sailor's way.*
>
> *I've crossed the Line and Gulf Stream, been round by Table Bay*
> *Around Cape Horn and home again, for that's the sailor's way.*
>   (THE SAILOR'S WAY)

Several writers quote the series of globe-trotting ships on which Yankee Jack sailed and, as has been shown, the dates of signing on and off for several of them are known from his discharge papers or can be gleaned from crew-lists, log books and the reports in *Lloyd's List* – but by no means all. At this point in his history, John is about to give up the deep-sea life of a shellback and return to the 'home trade', so it is appropriate to consider the other deep-sea ships he is known to have sailed on but for which there are no specific dates. Michael Bouquet is the primary (and much quoted) source of the list of ships, having closely inspected John's discharge papers and having talked to him at length. The list appears in Michael's own notebooks, in his writings, and in the list he supplied to Stan Hugill. Short's ships are also quoted in the various articles and newspaper reports that have been written over the years. The list itself is consistent (although present research has proved it to be incomplete) but the order in which the ships are quoted differs from source to source: a complete sequence cannot be deduced with certainty in this way.

After taking the recorded exact dates, fitting the known approximate dates in between and as far as possible putting his ships in order from crew returns, there are still three ships on which John is reported as having sailed but which, thus far, it has not been possible to place definitively in the sequence: *Feliza, Jane Gray,* and *Mary Ann.*

Feliza

There is no report of *Feliza's* destination when John was aboard her and hence no guidance as to how long his voyage may have been. *Feliza* is not listed in *Lloyd's Register* after 1855, and the *Mercantile Naval List*, where she does remain listed until lost in the North Sea in October 1860, gives no voyage details. There is only a fragmentary record of her voyages that can be gleaned from *Lloyd's List*.

It has been established that there is a gap in John's record between 22nd November 1857, and 29th October 1858. All *Feliza's* known voyages from 1857 to 1859 were to North-east Canada (to Quebec or Miramichi) and took in the order of 4-6 months from the start of one round trip to the next. The first that he could have sailed on left Swansea on 13th December 1857, and there is also time for a subsequent voyage (although none is noted in *Lloyd's List*) before the next, which did not finish until after the gap in John's record.

Thus, although it is not possible to give precise dates, it would seem that John's voyage on *Feliza* was to Canada and came between his trips on *Cezimpra* and *Hugh Block*, as previously discussed.

Jane Gray

Throughout the research for this book, Michael Bouquet, a reservoir of information that he had gleaned direct from John Short, has almost invariably been a reliable source. John Short told Michael that he had 'sailed in *Jane Gray* to Rio' (it is unclear, but probably also irrelevant, whether this refers to the Rio Grande of the Mexican border, Rio de Janeiro or the Rio Grande de Sul in Brazil). Michael certainly believed this *Jane Gray* to be, among several ships of that name, the vessel of Blythe (official no. 8522).

This *Jane Gray* sailed to Rio on various voyages: October 1856 to April 1857 (which was before John even sailed on the *Promise*), May 1858 to January 1859 (which would have overlapped his voyage on the *Hugh Block*), June 1861 to end 1861/early 1862 (when he was on the *George Washington*). She may also have called at Rio on her next trip but we know from the Crew List that John was not on that voyage.

There are two possible windows of opportunity in her history for John's reported voyage. The first is between October 1862 and October 1863 – but we know that during this period he was, sequentially, on board *Woodcote*, *Benjamin Buck Greene* and *Queen of the South* and so it can be discounted. The second possible period is between September 1864 and May 1866. John was discharged at Liverpool in September 1864 (*Levant* docked on the 10th) and his whereabouts are then uncertain until 6th May 1866 when he signed for a second trip on the *Benjamin Buck Greene*.

Lloyd's List shows that *Jane Gray* made a voyage to South America, including Montevideo, which was preparing to sail from Liverpool on 10th September 1864. This is almost certainly the voyage we are seeking, although there is no further detail on *Jane Gray* voyages in *Lloyd's List* until November 1866 when she arrives at Harvre from Blythe. From 1866 onwards her voyages were confined to European destinations in the Baltic and the Mediterranean.

The crew list from the *Benjamin Buck Greene* (for her voyage of May 1866 to January 1867 – John's second on board her) shows that his immediately previous voyage had been on the *Levant*. The likelihood is therefore that after his first trip on *Levant*, John next sailed on *Jane Gray* to Rio, and possibly on a subsequent vessel before re-joining *Levant* for a second voyage, after which he returned to the *Benjamin Buck Greene* for his second trip on her to Mauritius.

Mary Ann

This vessel presents a different and potentially difficult problem. Michael Bouquet is, as so often, the source. He noted that John Short sailed to New Brunswick to load timber on board the *Mary Ann*. Michael identifies her as the *Mary Ann*, official no. 48207, which was built in 1863 in New Brunswick, Canada, duly registered at St. John, and was 427 tons burthen.

According to the Canadian Heritage Information Network (C.H.I.N.), this *Mary Ann* made only two voyages. The first, from March to October 1864 was from St. John to Trinidad, Havana, then across to Greenock, on the Clyde, and back to St. John. The second, with a new owner (McLean) and a new master (Delaney), sailed from St. John on 28th August 1866, to Liverpool where she arrived on 24th October. She left on 2nd of November sailing for Trinidad but met bad weather – and worse. The *Lloyd's List* entry of 14th December gives the details:

> 'Skibbereen. 12th Dec. The *Mary Ann* (barq.), of St. John N.B.,
> Delaney, from Liverpool to Trinidad de Cuba, with coal, sprung her
> foremast in a gale from the westward on the morning of the 7th Dec.
> and in another gale in the night of the 9th she sprang a leak and went
> down off Cape Clear next day; crew saved.'

The report from Skibbereen is somewhat final! The vessel's registry was closed on January 8th 1867. John could not have been on either of these voyages: his discharge papers have shown that during the first he was on *Levant* and during the second he was on *Benjamin Buck Greene*.

Notwithstanding the incontrovertible evidence from the Skibbereen report, a vessel called *Mary Ann*, built in 1863, of 427 tons, registered at New Brunswick, owned by McLean and captained by Delaney, continues to appear in the *Lloyd's Register* each year until 1874 – the only difference being that she is described as barque-rigged rather than ship-rigged. It is, of course, entirely possible that, having lost the *Mary Ann* (no. 48207) in December 1866, McLean had another *Mary Ann* built – and *Lloyd's Register* does not give ships' official numbers. Nevertheless, it would be a strange coincidence that both vessels should have identical details, save the rig. It was probably these incorrect, un-amended entries in Lloyd's Register that deceived Michael Bouquet into identifying *Mary Ann no. 48207* as John Short's ship.

John's voyage, on whichever *Mary Ann* it was (there are nearly 300 of that name in the Canadian registry of the time), lies between 1863 and 1874. The periods within these limits when John is not known to have been on another vessel are: from September 1864 to April 1866 (however, the indications, as argued above, are that John was probably on *Jane Gray* and subsequently *Levant* during this period – although there may be time for him to have sailed on a *Mary Ann* between these two), and from September to December 1869, for we know he was back in the home trade after that. This would give enough time to sail for New Brunswick and back! It seems most likely that John sailed on both *Mary Ann,* and *Jane Gray* in the period between his voyages on *Levant,* i.e. between 14th September 1864 and the voyage which ended in May 1866.

So it is now possible, tentatively, to give an approximate sequence, although not a certain chronology, to all the deep water ships that John Short is known to have sailed on. The sequence with definite and approximate dates, and the known history of those ships, is given in Appendix 1.

Just as there are ships for which the records lack details, so there are claims about events and voyages to places which are not linked to specific ships. The *Somerset County Gazette,* in John's obituary article, stated that 'During his deep-sea sailing days, Mr. Short was a member of the crew of two vessels which came into collision in the Atlantic. One vessel was lost with all hands.' Two possible scenarios present themselves here:

1)   That a collision, as described, with the loss of one ship with all its crew did occur – in which case we have no idea which ship John Short was on (although obviously not the one that was lost with all hands), nor the identity of the vessel with which it collided.
2)   That the incident referred to was actually the collision, off the Old Head of Kinsale, of the *Queen of the South* with *Crescent* on 24th April 1864, as detailed above, where one vessel *was* totally lost although in reality the crew was saved. This is the most likely root of the *Gazette's* story, duly embellished, or misreported, in which case there is no need to seek further for the incident.

In another article, the claim is of 'a deep-sea career which took John Short to every major port in the world, from the South Seas to Arctic Russia.' If this is not just hyperbole, then we have yet to discover which ship took him to Arctic Russia - certainly not *Feliza* or *Mary Ann* - nor any other ship he is known to have sailed on. As usual, let us consider all the possibilities! The closest John could have got to Arctic Russia on any known vessel was if, in contradiction to the analysis made about *Jane Gray* above, he sailed on her not to Rio but, in the timber trade, into the furthest reaches of the Baltic where *Jane Gray* did go regularly from June 1868 until around October 1871. There is an almost complete sequence of half-yearly returns for *Jane Gray* from January 1866 to November 1871 and John Short does not appear in any of the crew lists. There is one gap in the sequence of returns where another voyage might have taken place, between 7th October 1869 and 17th April 1870. However, we know that before the end of 1869 John was home in Watchet and sailing on a local coaster so he could not have sailed on *Jane*

Gray at that time. In any case, he himself had said that it was to Rio that he sailed on *Jane Gray*.

Similar claims have John sailing 'to New Brunswick to load timber.' This may well refer to either his first voyage, on *Promise*, or to a later voyage on *Feliza* or *Mary Ann* as discussed above. Lastly, John is reported to have sailed 'to Mobile Bay to load cotton.' Certainly, several of John's shanties stem from cotton-stowing jack-screw chants of the cotton ports (although that does not mean he must have learnt them there). The voyage 'to Mobile' could have been almost any of his transatlantic voyages to South America, as Mobile was a staging post in voyages as well as a destination in its own right. Despite there being no evidence of any of his voyages being specifically to Mobile or to load cotton, we probably need to look no further, for there are no other time periods when Yankee Jack could have sailed there on other unknown vessels.

It is likely that both the 'Arctic Russia' and 'Mobile Bay to load cotton' references are spurious.

1869 – 1870

Paid off from the *Conference* in Bristol on 4th September 1869, John made his way, as so often before, home to Watchet. This seems to be the point at which he decided to give up deep-water sailing and return to his home port permanently. It may also be that a certain lady, whom we shall meet before long, had something to do with his decision.

> *It's of a young sailor who sailed the ocean blue*
> *He gained the good will of his captain and crew*
> *He sailed into harbour, one night for to lie*
> *And that was the beginning of one true love and I*
>
> *Well, it's home, dearest home,*
> *And it's there I like to be,*
> *Home for a while in me own country*
> *Where the Oak and the Ash and the bonny Elum tree*
> *They're all a-growing greener in the West Country*
> (HOME, DEAREST HOME)

By the end of the year, John Short - Yankee Jack - was sailing on *John* of Watchet and he remained with her until 9th June 1870. He probably then made one short trip on *Fortitude* before, on 21st July, he took over as Master of *Charles Phillips*.

These three vessels, like *Hawk* and *Telegraph* which followed, were small 'Home Trade' coastal vessels – *Hawk*, at 71 tons, was the biggest.

Since the Merchant Shipping Act of 1835, boats working in the home trade had been required by the Board of Trade to submit twice-yearly reports of their voyages, crews, and other details. Much of the detail of where John Short was and what he was doing over the ensuing decades, until 1900, comes from this source. Fortunately, most of his ships during this period had their home port at Watchet and were registered at Bridgwater. The biannual returns for these vessels are kept at the Somerset Heritage Centre (formerly the County Records Office). Different Owners and Masters were, however, not always rigorous as far as accurately completing these returns: in one consecutive sequence of five half-yearly returns, a John Short is recorded as having been born in five different years between 1840 and 1853. In this instance other details confirm it is the same John Short throughout, but some care has to be exercised as there were other John Shorts who had been born in the Williton registry district - in 1830 (Yankee Jack's uncle) and 1848 (no relation) - and were seafarers.

The Home Trade was, by definition, not confined to the coasts of the largest British island – it included all UK coastal waters, North European and Baltic ports, Irish waters and the continental side of the English Channel. The 1880-1882 voyages of *Crystal Bell* are given in Appendix 4 by way of one example of the day-to-day voyages of such Home Trade vessels. These were not deep-ocean craft: with a crew comprising only the skipper, the mate, one AB and possibly a boy or a cook, they needed no shantyman – whose purpose at sea was to co-ordinate the efforts of larger crews in handling cargoes, setting sails, raising the anchor or pumping her out. In later years John was to say that he preferred the barques, brigs and ketches that from now on would occupy his labours.

1871 - 1873

John only stayed with *Charles Phillips* until just before Christmas 1870 and then, on New Year's Day 1871, according to the returns, he signed as Mate on *Hawk*. John is, of course, missing from the 1871 census – he is, once more, at sea. His parents, Richard and Mary, are still living in Swain Street, now with four daughters, a son and two grandchildren.

Why John gave up the captaincy of *Charles Phillips* is unclear, but he stayed with *Hawk,* according to the crew returns, for a year and a half until 30th June 1872. It may or may not be significant that his signing on and off *Hawk* is recorded as being on the commencement and termination dates of the half-yearly returns – they may be generalisations rather than exact dates.

John almost certainly next joined *Friends*. The July to December return for 1872 has him joining her on 19th October, and the 1873 returns have him joining on 30th June 1872 – the same day he left *Hawk*. However, the latter date is probably incorrect, as the Crew return for the *Telegraph* indicates that John was on that boat from August until 19th October. *Hawk* and *Telegraph* (and *Electric*) were all owned by the Stoate family of Watchet; it is most likely that John simply moved from one of their vessels to the next as need and voyages determined. The inconsistencies of the crew returns frequently present such potential conflicts and one can do no more than reach a conclusion based on probability! Certainly, he was Mate on the *Friends* from 19th October onwards.

Ever since the *Friends* had been built in 1852, she had been owned by Llewellyn Hole, and John's father Richard had been her Master. She was one of four boats of that name registered at Bridgwater (later there would be five). She was the boat on which Sydney, having returned to Watchet, served as Mate under his father, before taking up his own captaincy. Now John would serve under his father again, as he had when he first went to sea all those long years ago, and things were about to change radically for the deep-sea sailor – he was planning to marry.

1873 July

On 23rd July 1873, at the parish church of St. James in Taunton, John Short married Anne Marie Wedlake. Anne Marie's sister, Clara, and John Mattocks Chapman were witnesses to the marriage which was conducted by the vicar, William Thomas Redfearne. The marriage certificate gives John and Anne as both resident at Rowbarton, Taunton. Why this should be their residential address at the time is unclear – it may be that Anne was in service there, but that would not account for it being John's residence. Anne (or Annie) came from another Watchet seafaring family: her mother's name was Mary Ann (née Browning, b.1833) and her father was Cpt. George Wedlake (b.1826). Annie had been born in 1846 and was 7 years John's junior. John, a God-fearing and sober man as already noted, followed at least in part the advice of the old salt in the forebitter *Go To Sea No More*.

> *Come all you bold seafaring men and listen to my song*
> *When you come off of them long trips, I'll have you not go wrong*
> *Take my advice and drink no strong drink*
> *Don't go sleeping with no whores*
> *Get married lads, and have all night in*
> *And go to sea no more.*

No more, no more,
And go to sea no more
Get married lads
And have all night in
And go to sea no more
(GO TO SEA NO MORE)

In actuality, John still did go back to sea, but his worldwide roving days were now over. He had a new wife, to whom he would prove totally dedicated, and spending time with her whenever his boat was home in Watchet must have been very attractive.

Throughout the rest of his life John remained proud of his deep-water sailing days and what he had done. He was conscious of the fact that most of his local contemporaries had not seen much of the world: Cecil Sharp noted that John had told him, 'It's no use going down to they chaps. They've never been out of the smoke (smell) of the farmyard.' He was also proud of his shanty repertoire - exceptional even among those who had sailed the world for, as he said, 'There was not so many as was travelling as I was as can remember them songs.'

1873 – 1880

John stayed with *Friends* for many years. He and Annie tried to start a family. The 1911 census posed a new question for the first time, namely, how many children had been born in a family and how many were still alive. In the census return for that year John and Annie record that they had had three children, although two had died without ever appearing in any pre-1911 census returns.

Subsequent research amongst the records of births and deaths reveals that George Wedlake Short (given his mother's maiden name as his middle name) had been born to John and Annie on 6th May 1874 and had died of diarrhoea on 1st October that same year – barely five months old. On 1st September 1879, Annie gave birth to another son, who was also christened George Wedlake Short, and he would survive to maturity.

It has not been possible to identify the third child cited in the 1911 census. Various children with the surname Short appear in the censuses between 1871 and 1911 and all can be attributed to families other than John and Annie's. There are no other individuals with the surname Short, who were both born *and* died in the Williton registry district between 1869 and 1900. It seems probable that the third child (possibly still-born) was born and died unregistered, but was nevertheless enumerated by John and Annie in the 1911 census.

1881 – 1884

As 1880 became 1881, John was still sailing on board the *Friends*, having served on her since 1872 but, on 23rd of March, he left her to join the *Crystal Bell* at Barnstaple as mate, for the princely wage of £4 per week. She was owned by George Passmore, registered at Bridgwater and, at 94 tons, was the biggest of the thirty-seven ships recorded at that time as having Watchet for their home port. Why John suddenly changed ship to serve on the *Crystal Bell* is not known; the wage is unlikely to have been any different; the owner and master had not changed; the size of the crew was the same; the voyages were perhaps a little further afield but not dissimilar – perhaps he was simply doing a favour for somebody.

In the census, on 3rd April 1881, when John is aboard the *Crystal Bell* at Northam, on the Torridge estuary in North Devon, his wife Annie Marie is recorded as the head of the household in Templar's Square, Watchet, living with their new son George and Annie's sister Clara Wedlake. Clara was probably there to help Annie who suffered hugely from rheumatoid arthritis, and as a result of which she was completely bed-ridden in her later years.

The *Crystal Bell* had a crew of three: the master was William Organ (22), the mate was John Short (42) and the third member of the crew was Joseph Burns – the 16 year-old cook. John stayed with the *Crystal Bell*, plying her trade to Cardiff, Charlestown, Antwerp, Newport and Cork throughout the year until 21st December when he left her at Paignton 'to join nother ship' as it says on the half-year return. This may be due to the *Crystal Bell* changing ownership for, although William Organ would remain as Master, the return for the first half-year of 1882 show Coomes of Paignton as the new owner. Richard Coomes had purchased the vessel following her seizure against a debt owed by George Passmore.

The 'nother ship' was, in fact, *Friends* to which John returned, although by now James Stadden, formerly the AB, had taken his place as Mate. Thus for the first half of 1882 John Short is on the crew as an AB and it was not until Stadden left, around the middle of the year, that John resumed his former position.

John now stayed as Mate on the *Friends*, under the captaincy of his father, until 14th August 1883 when both were discharged, together with the AB Alfred Short (no relation), and all three were replaced with a new crew. There is no apparent reason for their discharge after so many years on the *Friends*; still owned by Llewellyn Hole, she had certainly not changed ownership. It may be that John's father Richard, who was now nearly seventy, decided to give up the sea and that John decided to leave the *Friends* at the same time.

Whatever the reason, John transferred to William Stoate's 45-ton coaster *Electric* on which he served as Mate between August 1883 and March 1884 and from which, on the 18th, he transferred to *Telegraph*. This is the same boat on which he had made a previous trip back in 1872 and, as then, she was also owned by William Stoate. John appears on both the *Telegraph's* half-yearly returns for 1884, but is no longer listed in 1885.

1885 – 1891

In 1904, a testimonial for John Short from John Thorne - general merchant and boat-owner of Watchet - states that John had served on his boat the *Friends* (official no. 21552) for 'over two years.' This is a different boat to the *Friends* on which he served from 1872 to 1883 which was no. 10918. (Official Numbers, issued from 1855 onwards, were unique to each boat: even if a boat was renamed, she retained her official number and if a boat ceased to exist, for whatever reason, the number was never reissued to another boat.) In the January to June 1887 return, he is Mate on John Thorne's *Friends* and the return indicates he was also on board in the previous half-year although there is no documentation for that period. John was discharged from the *Friends* no. 21552 on 24th April 1887, so 'over two years' would take John's joining back to early 1885 just after he left the *Telegraph*.

From the latter half of 1886 until the end of 1891, a John Short appears on the crew list returns of the *Fortitude*. These records show the difficulties sometimes encountered in understanding the half-yearly returns: although the John Short listed is undoubtedly the same individual throughout these returns (he is listed as both 'previous' and 'continuing' or 'remaining'), his year of birth is variously given (or calculated from a stated age) as '40, '46, '49, '50 & '53. It is just possible that this is the John Short born in Watchet in 1848 – in which case we have no record of our 'Yankee Jack' between April 1887 and 1891.

However, it seems most likely that this *is* Yankee Jack, for the other John Shorts are identifiable on other boats during this period. There remains the potential problem of Yankee Jack's appearing on the returns of both the *Friends* and the *Fortitude* between July 1886 and June 1887, but it is entirely possible that he sailed on both periodically as voyages allowed. Certainly Yankee Jack was in the crew of a different boat by March 1891.

1891 March/April

In the census of 5th April, in Templars Square nothing has changed: Annie Marie is still recorded as the Head of the household with both George and Clara on the return. Clara had married Albert Williams, a paper-maker at the local mill, on October 11th 1884 but may still have been tending her sister Annie Marie while John was away. At the time of the census John was at Charlestown in Cornwall aboard *Annie Christian*.

ANNIE CHRISTIAN by THOMAS CHIDGEY © *Market House Museum, Watchet*

Isaac Allen was the owner and master of *Annie Christian* and John Short was sailing as Mate. Also in the crew were AB Henry John Norman (21) and Arthur Davis (15) the 'boy' (and cook). The story of how they only just got Charlestown is, in itself, a striking example of the sort of difficulties that even coastal vessels faced as they went about their trade. The tale was recounted over thirty years later by Henry John Norman – by then a Watchet master mariner in his own right – and reported in the *Somerset County Gazette* of 15th April 1933:

> 'We set out, four of us – Isaac Allen, the owner and master; John Short, mate; Alfred Davis, cook; and myself – in a little ketch called *Annie Christian*, which comes here now under another name. [*ADE*, see appendix.1] We were on a voyage with coal to Charlestown, in St. Austell Bay, Cornwall and we got as far as Land's End when a

severe blizzard came on from the north-east, and we failed to get shelter at Mount's Bay. In our company was a schooner with both masts gone. That will give you an idea of the weather! We drove off the coast from 50 to 60 miles with scarcely any canvas left.

'After the storm abated we got up what canvas we had left, and proceeded to return to land with all the warps lying about the deck in knots as a result of the heavy sea shipped. The sky-light was broken and water came into the cabin. There were mountainous seas 20 to 30 feet high and the galley, or cookhouse, was lifted by the water on deck to the top rail and fell back on deck again. After two or three days we arrived at St. Austell Bay. We were all frost bitten, and the captain hurt his ribs as a result of the breaking of the main gaff. People at Charlestown wondered how we reached there at all.'

There's a heavy storm a-rising, see how it gathers round
While we poor souls on the ocean wide are fearing to be drowned
There's nothing to protect us, love, or keep us from the cold
On the ocean wide where we must bide like jolly seamen bold
(ADIEU SWEET LOVELY NANCY)

Now the storm is over,
And we are safe on shore,
We will drink strong ale and brandy,
And we'll make those taverns roar,
We'll make those taverns roar, my boys,
We'll make those taverns roar,
And when our money is all gone,
We must go to sea for more.
(SWANSEA TOWN)

A testimonial given for John Short from Isaac Allen in 1904, states that John Short served on *Annie Christian* for two years. These would have been the years 1891 and 1892.

1892 - 1898

John now once again disappears from the crew lists for Bridgwater boats for a protracted period and it has not been possible to pinpoint him anywhere else until 1898. In the meantime, maritime activity and law were undergoing yet more changes and developments.

1894 saw the introduction of a new Merchant Shipping Act. The title of the act - *"An Act to consolidate Enactments relating to Merchant Shipping" [25th August 1894]* – was precise, but somewhat understated the reach of the Act. It was a major piece of legislation which encompassed everything from passenger conditions to lighthouses; from fishing boats to licensing pilots; from boat ownership to seaman's conditions, and effectively consolidated the numerous other acts that had been passed separately on different aspects of trade and function. In doing so, it also fully repealed the 25 Merchant Shipping Acts that had been introduced between 1852 and 1892 as well as Acts such as The Passengers Act [1852], The Foreign Deserters Act [1852], The Seaman's Savings Bank Act [1856] and The Admiralty Court Act [1861]. The 1894 Merchant Shipping Act defined a daily allowance of lime or lemon juice to counter scurvy and led, as John Short was at pains to explain to Cecil Sharp, to British vessels being known as 'limejuice ships' and ultimately to British sailors – and then other Britishers – being called 'limeys'.

'Serving out of Anti-Scorbutics

(6.) The lime or lemon juice shall be served out with sugar (the sugar to be in addition to any sugar required by the agreement with the crew).
(7.) The anti-scorbutics shall be served out to the crew so soon as they have been at sea for ten days; and during the remainder of the voyage, except during such time as they are in harbour and are there supplied with fresh provisions.
(8.) The lime or lemon juice and sugar shall be served out daily at the rate of one ounce each per day to each member of the crew, and shall be mixed with a due proportion of water before being served out.'

[MERCHANT SHIPPING ACT 1894]

The Act was even celebrated, if cynically, in the sailor's forebitter briefly quoted in the Introduction and which was also sometimes used as a capstan shanty:

If you want a merchant ship to sail the seas at large
You won't have any trouble if you've got a good discharge
Signed by the Board of Trade – and everything's exact
There's nothing in a limejuice ship contrary to The Act

Hurrah, boys, hurrah, I'll tell you it's a fact
There's nothing in the merchant ship contrary to The Act
Hurrah, boys, hurrah, sound the jubilee
Damn and bugger your merchant ships, they're ships of slavery

When you sign on board of a merchant ship you'll hear the articles read
They tell you of your beef and pork, your butter and your bread
Your sugar, tea and coffee, your peas and beans exact
Your lime juice and your vinegar boys, according to The Act

(THE LIMEJUICE SHIP)

1898 - 1900

John Short joined the *Josephine Marie,* as Mate, on 30th November 1898 and, according to the return, immediately prior to that he had been on the *Albert*, a ketch registered at Plymouth but owned by Alfred Nicholas at Watchet. We have not been able to discover how long he had served on the *Albert*. The *Josephine Marie's* previous Mate, Cornelius Allen, had drowned in an accident at Lydney Docks, Gloucestershire, on 27th July that year. Owned by the Besley family, and mastered by James Wilkins, the *Josephine Marie* was a coaster of 94 tons.

John would stay with the *Josephine Marie* throughout the next two years until she was destroyed, in harbour, at the end of 1900. The entry on the official return for the second half of the year records:

> 'On December 28th 1900 During heavy gale from North West the schooner Josephine Marie of Bridgwater collided with the schooner 'Hermatite' in Watchet harbour doing much Damage causing her to sink and become a total wreck. James Wilkins Master' [*sic*].

The entry fails to indicate the scale of the storm damage overall: in Sharp's notebook, from what John Short told him, he wrote: 'Harbour washed down. Five ships destroyed including the Mary Josephine [*sic*], Short's ship.' John's old ship *Friends* (10918) was another that was destroyed that night and, as Ben Norman records in his *Tales of Watchet Harbour*, the damage caused by the storm, in destroying the harbour and rendering it useless, meant that the consequent effect on commerce and trade in Watchet was little short of disastrous

HARBOUR WALL AND SHIPS DESTROYED – 29 TH DEC.1900
© Market House Museum, Watchet

1901

By the time of the 1901 Census, John and his wife had moved back to Market Street. Their son George, now 21, was also still living with them and had employment as a machine hand at the local paper mill. John is still recorded as a mariner. Clara has left the household and, it seems, had moved with her husband to the Bristol area.

Even after the loss of the *Josephine Marie*, and now well into his sixties, Yankee Jack still did not stay ashore. Cecil Sharp wrote in his field notebook that: "He [John Short] then became captain of Willie Horne's yacht at Minehead. The yacht capsized and four or five drowned which made Horne give up his yacht. Short wasn't on her at the time." That incident does appear to be the end of John Short's sailing career!

1902

The office of Town Crier in Watchet was in the gift of the Watchet Court Leet. Watchet had been a Borough from at least 1243 and the Borough Court or Court Leet was responsible for the smooth running of the town and ensuring that law and order were maintained, to which end they could try offenders and had a lock-up. The Court Leet now has no powers but meetings are still held annually, each

October at the Bell Inn, and the lock-up still exists behind the Museum which is housed in the 1819 Market House in Market Street.

According to local historian Ben Norman, the Court Leet appointed John Short as Town Crier in 1902 and he continued in the post for some time: in 1907 there is an entry in the Hobbler's Association record books for the sum of 1/- (one shilling in pre-decimal currency – equal to 5 new pence) paid to 'John Short cryer' on December 18th. There is a similar entry on 24th November 1910, and he was still fulfilling the role when Cecil Sharp visited him in 1914, for Sharp noted that: 'He is also Town Crier and gets 1/- for going up the street and might get a cry now and then. No doubt on account of his strong voice' - as quoted earlier, he could be heard two miles away!

There are further entries in the Hobbler Association's book for payments of 1/- in June 1915 and January 1916, but 'cryer' has become 'crier' and the recipient is not mentioned by name.

1904

In 1904, for reasons unknown, John was seeking testimonials as to his character. Michael Bouquet's notebooks reveal three that he received. The first came from Isaac Allen, still the owner and master of the *Annie Christian* – it read:

'May 30th 1904, Temple Villa Watchet. This is to certify that John Short of Watchet in the County of Somerset as serve as Mate on Bord thee Annie Christian of Liverpool for to years in a honest and faithfull seaman like manner, one cold be trusted. Isaac Allen. Master and Owner.' [*sic*] The two years seem to have been 1891 and 1892.

In December came two more testimonials: 'Steam Saw Mills. Watchet, Som. Dec 5. 1904. Memo from John Thorne and Son. Timber, Lime and General Merchants. This is to certify that John Short served in my employ for over two years and I have known him all his life as a steady honest man. R. T. Thorne.' The Thorne family were, as part of their business, also boat owners and owned the *Friends* (no.21552) on which John had sailed as Mate.

The second read: 'Watchet. December 12 1904. John Short of Watchet has applaid [*sic*] to us for a testimonial and we have very Great Pleasure in giving him one of Excellent Conduct he having been mate in our Employ for over 3 years, Sober Steady and attentive to his duties in every Respect and well fitted for any office on board of any vessel. W & J Besley, Shipowners.' [*sic*] Their ship had been the

Josephine Marie on which John had served from 30th November 1898 until she was destroyed in the gale of 28th December 1900.

At some point around this time, according to Rouse, John became a member of the Watchet Fire Brigade, of which he would in time become Captain. This may or may not be the reason he was seeking testimonials. I am grateful to Jim Nicholas, the curator of the Market House Museum in Watchet, for the information that the Parish Fire Service - i.e. of St. Decuman's – had been formed in 1855/56 and that the Watchet Station was probably a sub-station of that service. Further research is still required.

1905 – 1911

There is no further specific information on John's whereabouts or activity until the census of 1911.

In the census of 1911 only John and Annie live at the 5-room cottage in Market Street. George Short had married Alice Chidgey (b.1881) in the Parish Church of St. Decuman's on 25th August 1906 and they also now lived in a cottage in Market Street. One source claims that John and Annie 'had two children, George and Alice', but this is certainly an error – Alice was George's wife, not his sister. Alice's great niece has confirmed that George and Alice did not themselves have any children. As noted above, it is this 1911 census return that reveals the fact that John and Annie had had three children, of whom only one, the surviving George Wedlake Short, lived to maturity.

Despite his age, John remained sprightly and Taffy Thomas, the first UK Storyteller Laureate, recalls his grandfather Edward 'Teddy' Thomas, a native of Watchet, telling him that, as a boy, he and his friends would go down to the harbour after school and hear Yankee Jack singing. They would chat with him and he had a trick of swinging his leg up and over the quayside bollards to prove his agility even though he was in his eighties.

1914: April 20th – September 23rd

Cecil Sharp, the folk-song and dance collector, had been collecting material in the area since he was inspired to start his work after hearing the singing of John England as he worked in the vicarage garden at Hambridge in 1904. Sharp had collected widely in Somerset, including both Minehead and Watchet, from then on. Many of Sharp's contacts came through the local clergy – and this was also true of John Short. He was recommended by the Rev. Alfred Allen Brockington who at the time was vicar of Carhampton with Rodhuish. Brockington had come to the parishes in 1911 from St. Mary's, Taunton, where he had been curate. Sharp stayed with Brockington and the two of them went together when Sharp first visited John Short.

JOHN SHORT & REV. BROCKINGTON. photo by Cecil Sharp, 1914 © EFDSS

Journalistic reports of the date on which they first met vary between April, July and 'the summer' of 1914. The records of the number of songs that were collected are equally variable, from '57' or '60 in three days' to '100 altogether'. In a letter to the Times, discussing the shanty *Shanadar*, the Rev. Brockington suggests that the first visit was when 'Cecil Sharp was staying at my home, Carhampton Vicarage, in July 1914, and we paid visits on three successive days to Mr. John Short, the town-crier of Watchet.' Brockington's memory was not totally accurate but, fortunately, Cecil Sharp's field notebooks verify the exact dates of his visits and the songs collected on each occasion.

The first visit was on 20th April 1914 when Sharp noted 8 songs. He visited subsequently on the 21st (7 songs), the 22nd (8) and then again on the 24th (4). In May, Sharp collected from John on the 4th (5), 5th (3) and 6th (2). In June he was back again on the 2nd (9), 3rd (5) and 4th (2). Either the April, May or June dates could have been Brockington's 'three successive days'. Sharp's subsequent visits were July 9th (2) and September 23rd (2). This gave a total of 57 songs (56 shanties and *Sweet Nightingale*) over 12 days of visits. The songs, together with their mss. numbers and the dates on which they were collected appear in App.1.

That first meeting arranged by Brockington was fortuitous: having come to the parish in 1911, he left in 1915 to serve as a Temporary Chaplain to the Forces, ministering to the soldiers of the Great War, and he would return to Watchet again only as a visitor in later years.

Several of Sharp's visits to John Short, according to Sharp's acolyte and biographer Maud Karpeles, were in the intervals between the Somerset dates of Cecil's lecture-recitals, when he would 'hurry off to Watchet, a small port on the Bristol Channel, where lived John Short, a chantey singer. Short liked to be near the sea when singing and so he and Cecil Sharp would sit side by side on the quay and John Short would sing happily through the noise of wind and waves while Cecil Sharp smoked his pipe and jotted down the tunes.'

This was evidently not always an easy task. For example, for *The Bully Boat*, Sharp records nine variations of the tune across only four verses!

> *Oh the bully boat is coming*
> *Don't you hear the paddles rolling*
> > *Rando, Rando, Hooray, Hooray*
> *The bully boat is coming*
> *Don't you hear the paddles rolling*
> > *Rando, Rando, Ray*
>
> *I walked out one morning*
> *For to hear the steamboat rolling*
>
> *The bully boat is coming*
> *Down the Mississippi flowing*
> > (THE BULLY BOAT / RANZO RAY)

And when writing down the tune to the shanty *Lowlands* (*Dollar and a Half a Day*) which has already been quoted, Sharp writes some bars of music several times, crossing them through, before finally noting 'I have no doubt but that this is correct'.

In many shanties, Sharp notes variations to the tunes. Across the whole repertoire of shanties, one can begin to see Short's idiosyncrasies – the way he uses triplets; his preference for certain crying-out phrases; the detail of some of the 'trills, turns and graces' that so fascinated Sharp, the musician.

If there is a frustration for the modern singer of such songs, it is that John often gave Cecil only a verse or two and then said 'and so on', explaining that 'you do put in what you've a mind to after that.' This is not laziness or lack of engagement on John's part - shanties were normally only ever sung as an adjunct to work and were improvised at the time they were sung – although usually within certain limits and drawing on a stock of commonplace lines. In some cases it is only from other collections that we can build what can be called a complete or authentic text although, these are sometimes (if not often) bowdlerised.

The exception to this generalisation is where John's text comes from a recognisable narrative folk-song such as *Banks of the Sweet Dundee* (for the shanty *Heave Away Me Johnny*), *Blow the Candle Out* (for *Do Let Me Go*) or *The Irish Girl/Yellow Meal/Mr. Tapscott* (for the tune *Can't You Dance the Polka* – originally called *Larry Doonan*). In these cases, it is the storyline that determines the text, drawn from published broadsheets of the songs – although additional verses could be added if necessary to complete the job. This was another skill of the shantyman – to pick the right song for the task in hand: with the correct rhythm and speed for the job, not too long lest the story is not completed (and the crew frustrated), and not too short (so that an excess of unrelated additional verses has to be used).

There are occasional telling details about John from the notes Cecil Sharp made in his field notebooks – several have already been quoted, but on one occasion Sharp wrote: 'He now does some work repairing sails, he likes the smell of a sail loft.' We also know that John sometimes passed his time making knot-work with old ropes.

1914 - 1920

Sharp wasted no time going to print. His last collecting visit to John Short was on September 23rd 1914. By the end of the year Sharp had published his book *English Folk Chanteys* which included both *Billy Riley* and *Won't You Go My Way?* - the two shanties that had been noted on that last visit.

> *Oh Billy Riley, little Billy Riley*
> *Oh, Billy Riley, Oh*
> *O Billy Riley, walk him up so cheer'ly*
> *Oh Billy Riley, Oh*

O Billy Riley, how I love your daughter
O Billy Riley, I can't get at her
(BILLY RILEY)

I met her in the morning
*   Won't you go my way?*
I met her in the morning
*   Won't you go my way?*

I asked that girl to marry
She said she'd rather tarry
(WON'T YOU GO MY WAY?)

Sharp's commentary on Short's ability as a singer has already been noted, but his opinion of Yankee Jack was even more profound for, in the introduction to *English Folk Chanteys*, Cecil wrote: 'He has the folk-singer's tenacious memory and, although I am sure he does not know it, very great musical ability… Mr. Short has spent more than fifty years in sailing-ships and throughout the greater part of his career was a recognised chanteyman, *i.e.* the solo-singer who led the chanteys. It would be difficult, I imagine, to find a more experienced exponent of the art of chantey-singing, and I account myself peculiarly fortunate in having made his acquaintance in the course of my investigations and won his generous assistance.'

JOHN SHORT. photo by Cecil Sharp, 1914 © EFDSS

The extent of Sharp's debt to Yankee Jack is also apparent: 'Counting variants, I have collected upwards of 150 chanteys, all of which have been taken down from the lips of old sailors now living in retirement… Fifty-seven of the chanteys in my Collection, and forty-six of those in this volume, were sung to me by Mr. John Short of Watchet, Somerset.' Thus 81% of the (coincidentally) 57 songs published in *English Folk Shanties* came from John - and it could have been more if Sharp's editorial policy had not ruled out a further four that John sang to him, for he records that 'I have omitted certain popular and undoubtedly genuine chanteys, such as "The Banks of the Sacramento", "Poor Paddy works on the Railway", "Can't you dance the Polka", "Good-bye, Fare you Well", on the ground that the tunes are not of folk-origin, but rather the latter-day adaptations of popular, "composed" songs of small musical value.' We may criticise this attitude on the part of the collector today but approaches to traditional music and its performers have changed a great deal since Sharp's time, and he was at least completely clear, according to his own lights, in the material he was seeking and recording at the time.

Sharp's admiration was not confined to John's singing but manifest in other ways too, as Allen Brockington was to recall in an article on Cecil Sharp written for the *London Mercury* of April 1928 – and often re-quoted by later writers: 'I remember when we were collecting folk-shanties from Mr. John Short of Watchet he asked Mr. Short about his wife. The sailor led us to a bedroom, where lay a sweet-faced smiling old lady, crippled and twisted by rheumatism. Cecil questioned her, and she told him John did everything for her, cleaning the house, cooking the food, carrying her from her bed to the parlour – that he was her sole attendant. Cecil said to Mr. Short, when we were out of the lady's presence and preparing to resume singing, 'Mr. Short, you are a very fine singer, but your greatest achievement is in the next room'.'

Cecil Sharp had, over the years, fallen out with several of his collaborators: it is beyond the scope of this text to detail these or examine the reasons, but it is worth highlighting that his relationship with the people who gave him songs was invariably less fraught. John Short and Cecil Sharp shared a bond and an appreciation of each other. In the notice of John's death which would appear in the *Times*, and which is quoted in full below, it says: 'He always spoke with affection of Cecil Sharp, to whom he owed his reputation as a singer.'

John's beloved Annie Marie died on 5th May 1918. She was aged 72 and her death certificate gave the cause of death as '1) Chronic gouty asthma. 2) Heart failure.' They had been married all but 45 years.

It was also around this time that John finally gave up the water. When he retired from the deep-sea life, he had returned to the Home Trade. From the Home Trade he had briefly taken on the captaincy of a local boat-owner's yacht. After that he continued as a Hobbler until, according to Tony James, he 'retired from Hobbling when nearly 80.'

1920s

The publication of *English Folk Chanteys* had brought John Short's existence to a wider public. Richard Runciman Terry (1865-1938) was a classically-trained musician, organist, choirmaster and musicologist who specialized in church music and the revival of Tudor music. His maternal grandfather, Walter Runciman, was a celebrated mariner and lighthouse-keeper and a significant influence on his grandson. R.R. Terry had published volume one of *The Shanty Book* in 1921 – he now visited John Short and did his own collecting from him (although he only gleaned one shanty that John had not already given to Cecil Sharp).

Terry published sixteen of John's versions in *The Shanty Book v.II* (1924) and included occasional criticism, often unjustified, of the way Sharp had published some of them. Terry had a low opinion of Sharp both as a musician (he did not have the elite status within classical circles that Terry enjoyed, although he had an apparently higher level of public acclaim because of his folk-song collecting and publications), and as someone knowledgeable about shanties and their use (although Sharp had expressly stated his ignorance in this area in his introduction to *English Folk Chanteys*). When *The Shanty Book v.II* was published, Terry sent John Short a copy 'with the compliments of the author' hand-written and signed across the top of the cover. It is now in the proud ownership of a former Watchet harbourmaster.

The one shanty that Sharp had not collected from John, and Terry had, was *Sing Fare You Well* – another shanty from America which almost certainly originated among Negro dock workers in the cotton ports of the Southern States.

> *Fare you well, I wish you well*
> *Hooraw and fare you well*
> *Fare you well till I return*
> *Hooraw sing fare you well*
> (SING FARE YOU WELL)

Sharp died in 1924, and John Short was to outlive him by nine years.

1928

Fourteen years after he had initially introduced his parishioner, John Short, to Cecil Sharp, the Rev. Allen Brockington, by now serving as a diocesan officiate in Liverpool and a prolific author writing on poetry and Christian mysticism, contributed to a correspondence debate in *The Times* newspaper on the shanty now usually called *Shenandoah* writing that:

> 'I visited Mr. Short again in 1928. My wife was with me, and I asked him to sing *Shanadar* for her benefit. He said: "I don't know as I like *Shanadar*." I wondered why he did not like the song, and then I remembered that we had omitted from the published book one line he had sung in 1914, on account of its – well, unsuitability. Mr. Short seeing a lady was present and being too old to change his words at a moment's notice, escaped from his embarrassment by saying that he did not like the song. Whereas in 1914, it was the only tune that, of his own proper volition, and without any remark from Cecil Sharp, he had praised.'

Perhaps, at nearly ninety years of age, John was not as quick to improvisationally amend verses as he had been in his youth, but he was being as sensitive and courteous as ever: the verse in question, which Cecil had duly noted in his notebook back in 1914, was:

> *Oh Shanadar, I love your daughter*
> *Hooray, you rolling river*
> *I love the place she makes her water*
> *A-ha, I'm bound away, on the wild Missouri*
> (SHANADAR)

It may be worth noting here that although this shanty is commonly called *Shenandoah,* its more usual appellation and pronunciation among English sailors was *Shanadar* or *Shanadore.*

1929

Ben Norman, the Watchet historian, recalled another telling detail about John Short in his book on Watchet harbour across the centuries: 'As a small boy the writer attended a concert held at the local Baptist Church Schoolroom and remembers John Short walking up to the stage to entertain his friends and neighbours. John was then over ninety years of age, white haired and frail, but upright and proud. He disdainfully brushed aside some well meaning ladies who attempted to arm him up the steps to the stage and here he really burst forth with a surprisingly powerful rendering of a sea chanty and also a lovely old song called The Sweet Nightingale.'

Sweet Nightingale was the one song that Sharp collected from him that was not a shanty (although Sharp initially noted it as a capstan shanty, he subsequently crossed that through - but by now it was in the field notebook). The song was evidently a favourite of John's: 'Tis not a shanty, but I often used to sing it on board' he was later quoted as having said. Who knows what songs John knew apart from his shanties? – but that was where, at the time, Cecil Sharp's focus had been.

1930 October

In October 1930, John was the guest of honour at the Watchet Court Leet's Annual Dinner. As the *West Somerset Free Press* reported: 'during the post-prandial proceedings he delighted the company with a version of one of the sea chanties with which he was so familiar.' and Michael Bouquet recalls that John also sang *Sweet Nightingale* on that occasion.

> *My sweetheart come along, don't you heard the fond song*
> *The sweet notes of the nightingale flow?*
> *You shall hear the fond tale of the sweet nightingale*
> *That sings in those valleys below*
> *As she sings in those valleys below*
> (SWEET NIGHTINGALE)

1933 April 9th

John Short died in the small hours of the morning of Sunday 9th April 1933, at his son's Market Street house - close to the harbour. He had been confined to the house, and frequently to bed, for a few months and had been cared for by his son George and George's wife, Alice. Although his health was failing, he remained alert to the last and died, as he had been born, just yards from Watchet harbour.

> *Old Stormey he is dead and gone*
> *To my way, yah, Stormalong*
> *From ocean blue where he was born*
> *Aye, aye, aye, Mr.Stormalong*
>
> *And now we'll sing his fun'ral song*
> *O, roll her over, long and strong*
> (OLD STORMEY)

67

The Times of the following Wednesday carried an obituary notice:-

MR. SHORT, THE CHANTYMAN

Mr. John Short, the most famous of all chantymen, died last Sunday at his home in Market Street, Watchet, Somerset. He was born in March 1838 [*sic*], and had attained the great age of 95. The Rev. Dr. Allen Brockington writes:-

Cecil Sharp and I visited Short first in July, 1914, when he sang to us, on three successive days, more than 60 sea-chanties, of which 13 had not appeared in any collection of sea-songs. John Short's versions of many of those that had appeared were worth publishing because they excelled the other versions in quality and exactness. He was a very natural musician. His voice was deep and of great power, and yet so flexible that "runs" and delicate sequences were always clearly sung. He had a rare sense of pitch and, of course, an extraordinary memory. He was the chief contributor to Cecil Sharp's book, "English Folk Chanteys", and he afterwards sang for Sir Richard Terry. He still retained his almost unimpaired ability to sing at the age of 92. "Shanadore" was one of his favourite songs, and he was also very fond of singing "The Sweet Nightingale", which, strange to say, he had not seen "in print". "Tis not a sea-song, but I often used to sing it aboard ship". He always spoke with affection of Cecil Sharp, to whom he owed his reputation as a singer, though he himself thought little of reputation and much of homely things.

All his seafaring life was spent in windjammers, and he had a prejudice against steamships, because they did not produce "real sailors". After his retirement from seafaring life he became the town crier of Watchet. His invalid wife, whom he nursed with the greatest tenderness and devotion, died about 14 years ago. It was only during the last few months of his life that he was confined to the house with a painful illness.

On 15th April, both the *West Somerset Free Press* and the *Somerset County Gazette* carried lengthy articles reporting John's death and both repeated the *Times* obituary. The *County Gazette* gave notice of the funeral. Both papers also reported extensively on John's funeral in their editions of the following Saturday.

1933 April 15th

So it was that on Easter Saturday, 15th April 1933, John Short was laid to rest. The cortège left the house in Market Street at 2.30 pm, the coffin draped with a Red Ensign – the flag of the merchant navy in which John Short had spent his whole working life. As it passed through Market Street and Swain Street to the Baptist Chapel where the first part of the proceedings took place, a radio could be heard through an open window. Coincidentally, and appropriately, it was broadcasting one of John's well-loved shanties, *Rio Grande*, the sound accompanying his last passage through the town.

> *I wish I was in Rio today*
> *O you Rio*
> *So pack up your donkey and get under way*
> *We're bound for Rio Grande*
> *And away for Rio, O you Rio,*
> *Fare you well my bonny young girls*
> *We're bound for Rio Grande*
>
> *Bucko sailors you'll see there*
> *With long sea-boots and close-cropped hair*
>
> *I think I heard the Old Man say*
> *Heave her round and then belay*
> (RIO GRANDE)

The funeral arrangements were in the traditional style, although there were few immediate family to carry out the offices. The official mourners were John's son George, his nephew Herbert Short (Mary Jane's son) and the husbands of two of Annie Marie's sisters - Joseph Bale (Mary Elizabeth's husband) and Alfred Willicombe (Lily's husband). The coffin was borne by four of Alfred and Lily's ... sons Frederick, George, Ernest and Reginald (see appendix 4 for details of the relationships). An organ voluntary was played as the congregation assembled, and the two hymns included in the service were *Rock of Ages* and *Hark, Hark, My Soul*.

The service at the Baptist Chapel was conducted by the minister Rev. Pryce Jones who, whilst recalling Yankee Jack's life, referred to his 'Christian character'; his regular church attendance; his associations with Brockington, Sharp and Terry; his life and his shanties, concluding with Tennyson's poem *Crossing the Bar*:-

Twilight and evening bell,
And after that the dark
And may there be no sadness of farewell
When I embark

For tho' from out our bourne, of time and place
The flood may bear me far,
I hope to see my Pilot face to face,
When I have crossed the Bar.
(CROSSING THE BAR - TENNYSON)

The attendance at the funeral was very large, with friends, neighbours, Masters and shipmates from several local boats, the Harbourmaster, Watchet R.N.L.I. - representatives, in fact, of the whole Watchet community. There were some twenty to thirty floral tributes, some from as far afield as Torquay and London, from Annie Marie's sister Clara in Bristol, and from Allen Brockington who was now living in Liverpool. Brockington had also written a letter of condolence to George: 'My wife and I are both deeply grieved to hear that your dear father and our dear friend has died. We have sent off a wreath as a token of our love for him and our sympathy with you. I shall never forget the happy hours I spent in his company, and I thank God that I was privileged to know him.'

Stormy's dead that good old man
*   Walk him along Johnny, carry him along*
Lay him down as best we can
*   Carry him to the burying ground*

And it's O, you Stormy
*   Walk him along Johnny, carry him along*
O, you Stormy
*   Carry him to the burying ground*

Of all the sailors he was the best
But now he's dead and gone to rest

No danger now from wreck or gale
He's moored at last an' furled his sail
(CARRY HIM TO THE BURYING GROUND)

The organist played *Rest in the Lord* as the coffin was carried from the chapel. The entire procession then moved to the parish church where John was buried - as Jack Hurley put it, 'at St. Decuman's, "the kirk upon the hill" of Coleridge's *Ancient Mariner.*' The Baptist minister again officiated and prayers were also offered by the Anglican vicar, the Rev. W. Burgess. The following evening, in the Baptist chapel, a memorial service was held. Sadly, the record of the exact location of John Short's grave within the churchyard is now lost.

Legacy

Slate plaque on the wall of 9 Market St., Watchet

Over the years, several journalists, historians, writers and activists have kept John's memory alive – those sources appear in the bibliography. Some of John's shanties, via Cecil Sharp, found their way into the Novello folk-song books that had regular school use from the 1920s onward. Several, of those that Cecil Sharp and Richard Terry had published, have been learnt and sung by generations of folk-singers and maritime song groups, although they have often been unaware of the source.

Local journalist and author, Tony James, one of the prime movers in the Watchet Boat Museum, who has written on occasion about John Short, was inspired by his story in naming a newly built 'flatner' – an historic flat-bottomed boat-type of the Somerset levels – *Yankee Jack*. Tony subsequently sailed *Yankee Jack* around the 'forgotten ports of the Southwest', and a book followed in 2006 further sustaining John's name.

9 Market St., Watchet – Yankee Jack's cottage

Samuel Taylor Coleridge had been inspired to write his epic poem *The Rime of the Ancient Mariner* in 1797 when he visited Watchet, walking from his home in nearby Nether Stowey, and in 2003 Watchet's Market House Museum commissioned Scottish sculptor Alan Herriot to create a sculpture of Coleridge's character, complete with albatross, to grace the promenade at Watchet. Five years later he was again commissioned by the Market House Museum, this time to create a statue of John Short. It was unveiled on 22nd March 2008 on the esplanade overlooking the harbour, with the assistance of the Watchet Town Band and a local shanty crew – John Short was back, surveying the massive changes that had happened to his home port over the years.

John's shanties, even those that Sharp and Terry did not publish, have not been forgotten either. In May 2011 a set of three CDs giving new recordings of the whole of John Short's repertoire, as given to Cecil Sharp and Richard Runciman Terry, was launched by S&A Projects and WildGoose Records – performed by an international crew of professional sea-song singers, and researched in depth by UmberMusic.

Alan Herriot's bronze of Yankee Jack

The days of the square-riggers are long gone – save in the sail training ships that several maritime nations now proudly boast – but the work songs of those times, the shanties, are remembered and sung in different contexts, and for different purposes, and the memory of John Short - Yankee Jack - shantyman and Watchet sailor, will live on as long as his songs are sung.

> *As I was a-walking down Watchet's Swain Street*
> *A jolly old shipmate I chanced for to meet*
> *Hello, brother sailor, you're welcome to home*
> *In season to Watchet, I think you are come.*
> (THE WATCHET SAILOR)

Appendix 1 ~ Short's shanties

The songs are listed according to the titles John Short used. More familiar titles and text or tune identification is given in brackets. Short often gave Cecil Sharp only a few verses; texts are therefore, where appropriate, elaborated from other texts of the same version. All John Short's verses are always included. Recent recordings of the songs were released on three CDs by WildGoose Records & S&A Projects in 2011 (WGS381, WGS382 and WGS388). Full notes on the recordings, and more detail of the origins of the shanties, can be found at www.umbermusic.co.uk/SSSnotes.htm.

A-roving
Billy Riley
Blackball Line, The
Blow Away The Morning Dew
Blow Boys Blow (Sacramento)
Blow Boys Come Blow Together
   (Blow, Me Bully Boys, Blow)
Boney Was A Warrior
Bulgine Run (Let the Bulgine Run)
Bull John Run, The (Eliza Lee)
Bully Boat, The (Ranzo Ray)
Bully In The Alley
Carry Him to the Burying Ground
   (General Taylor)
Cheerly Men
The Dead Horse (Poor Old Man)
Do Let Me Go
   (text: Blow the Candle Out)
Fire! Fire! (Fire Down Below)
Good Morning Ladies All
Handy My Girls (So Handy)
Hanging Johnny
Haul Away Joe
Haul On The Bowline
He Back, She Back
   (Old Moke Picking on a Banjo)
Heave Away My Johnny
   (We're All Bound To Go –
   text is Banks of the Sweet Dundee)
Hog eyed Man
Homeward Bound
 (Goodbye, Fare Thee Well)
Huckleberry Hunting (Me Ranzo Ray)
Hundred Years on the Eastern Shore
   (A Hundred Years Ago)

I Wish I Was With Nancy (tune : 'Dixie')
Johnnie Bowker
Knock A Man Down
   (Blow the Man Down)
Liza Lee (Yankee John Stormalong)
Lowlands (Dollar and a half a day)
Lucy Long
Mr. Tapscott
   (The Irish Girl OR Yellow Meal)
Old Stormey (Mister Stormalong)
One More Day
Paddy Doyle
Paddy Works on the Railway
Poor Old Man (Johnny Come To Hilo)
Ranzo (Poor Old Reuben Ranzo)
Rio Grande
Roll And Go (Sally Brown)
Rosabella (Saucy Rosabella)
Round the Corner Sally
Rowler Bowler
Santy Anna (Plains of Mexico)
Shallow Brown
Shanadore (Shenandoah)
Sing Fare You Well
So Early in the Morning
   (The Sailor Likes His Bottle O)
Stormalong John
Sweet Nightingale
Times Are Hard & The Wages Low
   (Leave Her, Johnny, Leave Her)
Tom's Gone To Ilo
Tommy's Gone Away
Whip Jamboree
Whisky Is My Johnny
Would You Go My Way

74

A-roving (Amsterdam)

mss. no.2892 coll.21/4/14

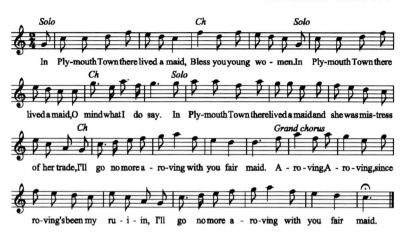

In Plymouth town there lived a maid   *Bless you young women*
In Plymouth town there lived a maid   *O mind what I do say*
In Plymouth town there lived a maid
And she was mistress of her trade
          I'll go no more a-roving with you fair maid
          A-roving, a-roving, since roving's been my ru-i-in
          I'll go no more a-roving with you fair maid

I took this fair maid for a walk
And we had such a loving talk

I put my arm around her waist
Says she young man you're in great haste

I put my hand upon her knee
Says she young man you are too free

I put my hand upon her thigh
Says she young man you're not too high

I lift the fair maid over the stile
And nine months after she had a little child

This girl she left me broke and bent
So back to sea I quickly went

75

Billy Riley

mss. no.3059 coll.23/9/14

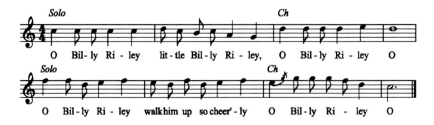

O Billy Riley little Billy Riley
O Billy Riley O
O Billy Riley walk him up so cheer'ly
O Billy Riley O

O Mister Riley, O Missus Riley
O missy Riley, screw her up so cheer'ly

O Billy Riley was a boarding house master
O Billy Riley had a lovely daughter

O Missus Riley, how I love your daughter
O missy Riley, I can't get at her

O Missy Riley, little Missy Riley
Oh missey Riley, screw her up so cheer'ly

O Billy Riley, haul and hang together
O Billy Riley walk him up so cheer'ly

The Blackball Line

mss. no.2879 coll.20/4/14

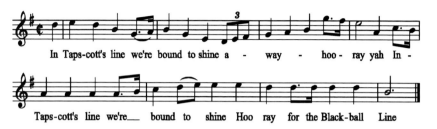

In Taps-cott's line we're bound to shine a - way - hoo - ray yah In -
Taps-cott's line we're___ bound to shine Hoo ray for the Black-ball Line

In Tapscott's line we're bound to shine
A-way-hoo-ray-yah
In Tapscott's line we're bound to shine
Hoo-ray for the Black-Ball Line

In the Blackball Line I served me time
In the Blackball Line I wasted me prime

Just take a trip to Liverpool
To Liverpool that Yankee school

Oh the Yankee sailors you'll see there
With red-topped boots and short-cut hair

O fifteen days is a Blackball run
But Tapscott's ships are a thousand ton

I'll bid those Blackball ships adieu
For Tapscott's ships are good and true

77

Blow Away The Morning Dew

mss. no.2891 coll.21/4/14

As I walked out one morning fair to view the meadows round, it's there I spied a
mai-den fair come trip-ping o'er the ground   O   blow   you winds of   mor-ning
Blow the winds I ho   Clear a-way the mor-ning dew say blow   boys   blow

As I walked out one morning fair to view the meadows round
It's there I spied a maiden fair come tripping o'er the ground
  O blow ye winds of morning
  Blow ye winds Hi! Ho!
  Clear away the morning dew
  And blow boys blow

My father has a milk-white steed and he is in the stall
He will not eat his hay or corn, nor will not go at all

When we goes in a farmer's yard and sees a flock of geese
We dang their eyes and cuss their thighs and knock down five or six

As I was a walking down by the riverside
It's there I saw a lady fair a-bathing in the tide

As I was a-walking, out in the moonlight
It's there I saw a yaller gel and her eyes they shone so bright

We strolled along until we came to a field of new-mown hay
She says young man this is the place for men and maids to play

As I was a-walking down Paradise Street
It's there I met old John de Goss, he said "Will you stand a treat?"

78

Blow Boys Blow (Sacramento)

mss. no.2890 coll.21/4/14

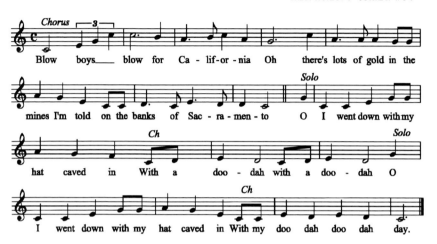

Blow boys blow for Ca - lif-or - nia Oh there's lots of gold in the mines I'm told on the banks of Sac - ra - men - to O I went down with my hat caved in With a doo - dah with a doo - dah O I went down with my hat caved in With my doo dah doo dah day.

Blow boys blow for California
Oh there's lots of gold in the mines I'm told
On the Banks of the Sacramento

Oh I went down town my hat caved in
With a doo dah, With a doo dah
Oh I went down with my hat caved in
With my doo dah doo dah day

Oh around Cape Horn in the month of May
Oh, around Cape Horn is a bloody long way

To Sacramento we will go
We're the bullies for to kick her through

Oh, round the Horn and up the line
Oh, we're the bullies for to make her shine

Breast your bars and break your backs
Heave and make your spare ribs crack

Around Cape Stiff in seventy days
Around the horn and back again

Blow Boys Come Blow Together
(Blow, Me Bully Boys, Blow)

mss. no.2898 coll. 22/4/14

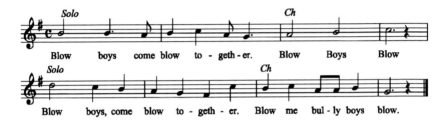

Blow boys come blow together
Blow boys blow
Blow boys come blow together
Blow my bully boys blow

A Yankee ship came down The River
Her masts and spars they shone like silver

'Twas a Yankee mate and a lime-juice skipper
They make her fly like a China clipper

And who do you think was the Master of her
Tommy Brown the big-bellied sinner

Who's the mate who knows no pity
Why Bully Bragg of New York City

And what do you think we had for supper
Belaying-pin soup and a roll in the gutter

What do you think we had for cargo
Shot and shell to break the embargo

Blow today and blow tomorrer
And blow me boys for better weather

Blow me boys and blow for ever
And blow her home to the London river

Boney Was A Warrior

mss. no.2945 coll.2/6/14

Boney was a warrior
Way ay yah
A bully fighting terrier
John Francois

First he fought the Rooshians
Then he fought the Prooshians

Bonny went to Moscow
Moscow was on fire O

We licked him well at Trafalgar
Blew away both mast and spar

Boney went to Elbow
Came back to make another show

Boney went to Waterloo
And there he met his over-throw

Boney went a-cruising
On board the Billy Ruffian

Boney went to Saint Helen
Boney ne'er came back again

Boney broke his heart and died
In Corsica he should have stayed

Boney was a general
A rorty, shorty, general

Bulgine Run (Let the Bulgine Run)

mss. no.2900 coll.22/4/14

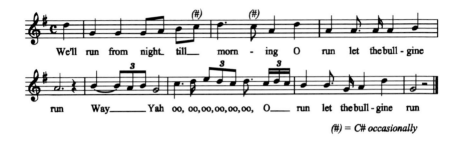

We'll run from night till morning
O run let the bulgine run
Way-yah oo, oo, oo, oo, oo, oo
O run let the bulgine run

We'll run from here to dinner time

We'll run from Dover to Calais

We'll run from York to London

O we sailed all day to Mobile Bay

We'll run down south around the Horn

From Liverpool to Frisco

Pump her dry and away we'll go

She's a dandy clipper and a bully crew

The skipper'll make her old nose bleed

We'll rock and roll her over

The Bull John Run (Eliza Lee)

mss. no.2999 coll.9/7914

I wished I was a fancy man
Ha he, ha ho, are you most done
I wished I was a fancy man
So clear the track let the bulgine run
With my hi rig-a-jig in a low-back car
Ha, he, ha, ho, are you most done
I wished I was a fancy man
So clear the track let the bulgine run

As I walked out one morning fair
I met miss Liza I declare

The day was fine and the wind was free
With Liza Lee all on my knee

Them London Julies hang around
And there my Liza will be found

Them Bow'ry girls I love so dear
With their slender waist and their golden hair

I'll take another girl on my knee
And leave behind Miss Liza Lee

Bully Boat, The (Ranzo Ray)

mss. no.2962 coll.4/6/14

Ah the bully boat is coming
Don't you hear the paddles rolling
Rando Rando Hoo-ray Hoo-ray
The bully boat is coming
Don't you hear the paddles rolling
Rando Rando ray

Ah the bully boat is coming
Down the Mississippi floating

As I walked out one morning
To hear the steamboat rolling

It's there I met a maiden and with
Baskets she was laden

O I'm bound away to leave you
And I never will deceive you

When I come again to meet you
It's with kisses I will greet you

Bully In The Alley

mss. no.2936 coll.6/5/14

So help me Bob I'm bully in the alley
Way ay bully in the alley
Bully down in an alley
So help me Bob I'm bully in the alley
Way - ay bully in the alley
Bully in tin pot alley
Way - ay bully in the alley

Sally is the girl down in our alley
Way - ay bully in the alley
Sally is the girl down in our alley
Way– ay bully in the alley
Have you seen our Sally
So help me Bob I'm bully in the alley
Way – ay bully in the alley
I could love her cheer'ly
Way – ay bully in the alley

Sally is the girl that I love dearly
Way – ay bully in the alley
Sally is the girl that I love dearly
Way - ay bully in the alley
She's the girl in the alley
So help me Bob I'm bully in the alley
Way – ay bully in the alley
Oh I spliced her nearly
Way – ay bully in the alley

I'll leave my Sally and go a sailing
Way - ay bully in the alley
I'll leave my Sally and go a sailing
Way - ay bully in the alley
I'll leave her in the alley
So help me Bob I'm bully in the alley
Way – ay bully in the alley
Going to go a-whaling
Way – ay bully in the alley

So help me Bob I'm bully in the alley
Way - ay bully in the alley
So help me Bob I'm bully in the alley
Way - ay bully in the alley

Carry Him to the Burying Ground
(General Taylor)

mss. no.2903 coll.22/4/14

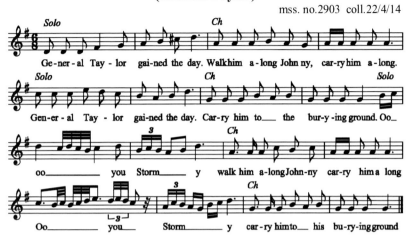

General Taylor gained the day
Walk him along Johnny carry him along
General Taylor gained the day
Carry him to the burying ground

Oo……….. you stormy
Walk him along Johnny carry him along
Oo……….. you stormy
Carry him to the burying ground

Then a-way-a you Stormy
Way-ay you Stormy

General Taylor died long ago
He's gone me boys where those winds don't blow

Dan o Connell died long ago
Dan he was an Irish boy-O

Wide and deep we'll dig his grave
His shroud of finest silk was made

I wished I was in Liverpool Town
Where them flash girls roll around

Cheerly Men

mss. no.2901 coll.22/4/14

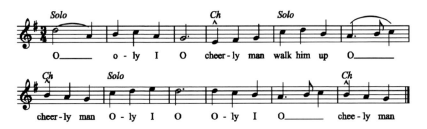

O_____ o - ly I O cheer - ly man walk him up O_____

cheer - ly man O - ly I O O - ly I O_____ chee - ly man

O Oly - I - O
Cheerly man
Walk him up, O,
Cheerly man
Oly I O, Oly I O
Cheerly man

O, to the cathead – I - O
O, shift the dead
Heavy as lead, heavy as lead

O, haughty cocks
O, split her blocks
O, on the rocks, on the rocks

O, rouse her and shake her
O, shake and wake her
O, we will make her; we will make her

The Dead Horse (Poor Old Man)

mss. no.2884 coll.20/4/14

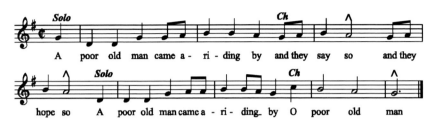

A poor old man came a-riding by
And they say so, and I hope so
A poor old man came a-riding by
O poor old man

Says I old man your horse will die
Says I old man your horse will die

And if he dies I'll tan his hide
And if he lives my horse I'll ride

As I was a rambling down the street
A flash young girl I chanced for to meet

Says I young girl won't you stand treat
O yes if you come to the bottom of the street

Off we went in a low back car
She took me to Jack Storey's bar

She call-ed for some cakes and wine
To plumb her well was my design

I plumbed her well and found she was grand
But now I've left her on the strand

Do Let Me Go (text: Blow the Candle Out)

mss. no.2958 coll.3/6/14

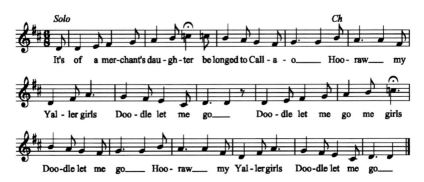

It's of a merchant's daughter belonged to Callao
Hoo-raw my yaller girls doodle let me go
Doodle let me go girls Doodle let me go
Hoo-raw my yaller girls doodle let me go

'Twas late last Saturday evening he went to see his dear,
Hoo-raw my yaller girls doodle let me go
The candles were all burning and the moon shone bright and clear
Hoo-raw my yaller girls doodle let me go

He went to his love's window, to ease her of her pain
She quickly rose & let him in and went to bed again

The street they are to lonely for you to walk about,
O take me in your arms love and blow the candle out

It's there they tossed & tumbled till daylight did appear
The sailor rose, put on his clothes, says fare the well my dear

Now if we prove successful, love, please name it after me
And if it is a boy then send the bastard off to sea

It was some six months after this young girl she grew stout
And often thought upon the time she blew the candle out

Fire! Fire! (Fire Down Below)

mss. no.2950 coll.2/6/14

Fire! Fire! Fire down be-low It's fetch the bucket of water girls there's fire down be - low

THE SAME TUNE IS USED FOR BOTH VERSE & CHORUS

Fire! Fire! Fire down below
It's fetch a bucket of water girls
There's fire down below.

There's fire in the galley, there is fire down below
Fetch a bucket of water of water girls, there's fire down below.
Fire, fire.

There's fire in the fore-top, there's fire in the main
Fetch a bucket of water girls and put it out again.
Fire, fire.

As I walked out one morning all in the month of June
I overheard an Irish girl singing this old song.
Fire, fire.

Fire in the lifeboat, fire in the gig
Fire in the pig-sty roasting of our pig
Fire, fire.

Fire in the windlass, fire in the chain
Fire in the foresheet and fire in the main
Fire, fire.

Fire up aloft boys, fire down below
Douse it out with water girls and let's roll and go

Good Morning Ladies All

mss. no.2904 coll.24/4/14

(INTRO)
Aye yo   Aye yo

I thought I heard the Captain say
Aye yo   Aye yo
O go on board your pilot boat and roll her down the bay
Ha Ha my yaller girls, Good morning ladies all

Our Captain on the quarter deck
He was looking very sad, He like a man was mad

O ladies short and ladies tall
O ladies I have had them all

Rock and roll her down the bay
We're homeward bound to spend our pay

When we get back to Bristol town
We'll make those flash girls waltz around

I thought I heard the Captain say
O go on board your pilot boat and roll her down the bay

Handy My Girls (So Handy)

mss. no.2952 coll.2/6/14

(INTRO)
So handy me girls so handy

Be handy in the morning
So handy my girls so handy
Be handy in the morning
So handy my girls so handy

For we are outward bound you know
For we are outward bound you know

Be handy with your washing girls
Why can't you be so handy O

My love she is a dandy, O
And she is fond of Brandy, O

O shake her and we ll wuku hur
Up aloft from down below

I thought I heard our Captain say
At daylight we are bound away

Bound away for Botany Bay
Farewell me girls we cannot stay

Hanging Johnny

mss. no.2946 coll.2/6/14

And they calls me hanging Johnnie
Hooray hooray
And they calls me hanging Johnnie
So hang boys hang

They hanged my poor old father
They hanged my poor old mother

Oh yes they hanged me mother
Me sister and me brother

They hanged me dear old Granny
They strung her up so canny

They say I hanged for money
But I never hung nobody

We'll hang this bloody sheet
Oh haul her up so neat

We'll hang him up forever
We'll hang for better weather

A rope, a beam, a ladder
I'll hang ye's all together

Haul Away Joe

mss. no.2899 coll.22/4/14

Haul a - way haul a-way haul a-way my Ro - sie Way haul a-way

haul a - way Joe O you talk a - bout your a - ver girls and

round the cor-ner Sa - lly Way haul a - way haul a - way Joe. Haul a -

INTRO
Haul away, haul away, haul away my Rosie
Way haul away, haul away Joe

O you talk about your Havre girls, and round the corner Sally
Way haul away, haul away Joe
But they cannot come to tea, with the girls on Booble Alley
Way haul away, haul away Joe

First I had a German girl, and she was fat and greasy
Then I had a Frenchie girl who took life free and easy

I got myself a Yankee girl who wasn't very civil
And then I had a Spanish girl who's worse than any devil

Once I was in Ireland a digging turf and tatties
Now I'm on a lime-juice ship hauling on the braces

Once I had an Irish girl and she was slow and lazy
But now I've got me Rosie and she nearly drives me crazy

Once I had a little dog, and his name was Toby
And he bit the crack out of poor little Rosie

Now up aloft this yard must go, we'll pull her free and easy
Another pull and then belay, we'll make it all so easy.

Haul On The Bowline

mss. no.2951 coll.2/6/14

INTRO
Haul on the bowline, O Kitty you are my darling
Haul on the bowline The Bowline haul

Because she had a fore-top, Fore and main and bowline
Haul on the bowline, the bowline haul
Because she had a main-top, main and mizzen to bowline
Haul on the bowline, the bowline haul
Haul on the bowline O Kitty you are my darling
Haul on the bowline, the bowline haul

Ten thousand miles to go boys, hauling on the bowline
Ten thousand miles and back again, hauling on the bowline

A mains'l and a tops'l, t'gans'l and a royal
A tops'l and t'gans'l boys a royal and a skys'l

We'll take this yard way up aloft, and hang her on a tree, O
Haul and break you backs and spread her wide and free.

96

He Back, She Back (Old Moke Picking on a Banjo)

mss. no.2960 coll.3/6/14

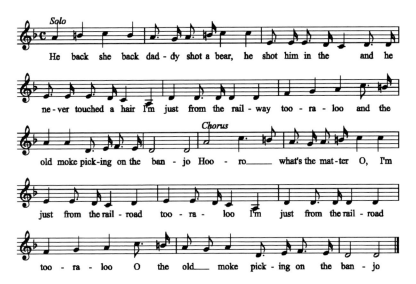

He back, She back, Daddy shot a bear
He shot him in the arse, and he never touched a hair   (stern)
I'm just from the railroad, too-ra-loo
O the old moke picking on the banjo
    Hoo-ro, what's the matter O
    I'm just from the railroad, too-ra-loo
    I'm just from the railroad, too-ra-loo
    O the old moke picking on the banjo

Roll her boys, bowl her boys, give her flaming gip
Drag the anchor off the mud and let the bastard rip

Rock-a-block, chock-a-block, heave the capstan round
Fish the flaming anchor up, for we are outward bound

Whisky O, Johnny O, the mud-hook is in sight
Tis a hell of a way to the girls that wait at the old Nantucket light

Pat get back, take in your slack, heave away me boys
Heave away me bully boys, why don't you make some noise

97

Heave Away My Johnny (We're All Bound To Go)
(text: Banks of the Sweet Dundee)

mss. no.2888 coll.21/4/14

It's of a farmer's daughter, So beautiful I'm told,
Heave away, me Johnny, heave away,
Her parents died and left her Five hundred pounds in gold
Heave away me bonny boy, we're all bound to go.

But there a wealthy squire who oft came her to see,
But Mary loved a ploughboy on the banks of the Sweet Dundee

Her uncle and the squire rode out one summer's day;
"Young William he's in favour," Her uncle he did say

Indeed 'tis my intention to tie him to a tree,
Or to bribe the press-gang, on the banks of the Sweet Dundee

The press-gang came to William When he was all alone,
He boldly fought for liberty, but they were six to one.

The blood did flow in torrents- "Pray, kill me now," said he,
"I would rather die for Mary, on the banks of the Sweet Dundee

This maid, one day, was walking, Lamenting for her love,
She met the wealthy squire down in her uncle's grove;

He put his arms around her; "Stand off, base man," said she,
"For you've banished the only man I love, from the banks of the Sweet
Dundee

Young Mary took the pistols, His sword he used so free,
Then she did fire, and she shot the squire, on the banks of the Sweet Dundee

Her uncle overheard the noise and he hastened to the ground
Since you have shot the squire I'll give you your death-wound!"

"Stand off, then," cried young Mary, "Undaunted I will be."
She the trigger drew and her uncle slew, on the banks of the Sweet Dundee

He willed his gold to Mary, who fought so valiantly,
Then he closed his eyes, no more to rise, on the banks of the Sweet Dundee

Hog eyed Man

mss. no.2924 coll.4/5/14

The hog-eye man is the man for me
He brought me down from Tennessee
> *And a hog eye, steady up a jig*
> *And a hog-eye, steady up a jig*
> *And all she wants is her hog eye man*

O the hog-eye men are all the go
When they come down to Frisco

He came to the place where his Sally did dwell
He knocked on the door and he rang her bell

Sally's in the parlour sitting on his knee
And all she wanted was a young hog-eye

O the hog-eye man is the man for me
For he sent me home with a big belly

It's who's been here since I've been gone
Some Yankee Jack with his sea-boots on

It's a hog-eye ship and a hog-eye crew
And a hog-eye mate and skipper too

Mary Ann and Sarah Jane
Is the two biggest whores in Whitemore Lane

Homeward Bound (Goodbye, Fare Thee Well)

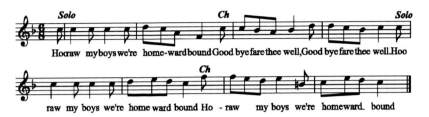

mss. no.2889 coll.21/4/14

Hooraw my boys we're homeward bound Good bye fare thee well, Good bye fare thee well. Hoo
raw my boys we're home ward bound Ho - raw my boys we're homeward bound

Hooraw my boys we're homeward bound
Good bye farewell, Good bye farewell
Hooraw me boys we're homeward bound
Hooraw me boys we're homeward bound

We're homeward bound don't you hear the sound
Man the capstan and breast her round

We're homeward bound I'll have you to know
It's over the water to England we'll go

O fare you well I wish you well
When we get back we'll raise merry hell

The anchors away and the sails they are set
The girls we are leaving we'll never forget

We're homeward bound and so they say
The hook on the cat-fall and run her away

We're homeward bound to Portsmouth Town
Where the girls will all come down

We'll spend our pay in one week ashore
And then we'll go to sea once more

Huckleberry Hunting (Hilo, Me Ranzo Ray)

mss. no.2927 coll.5/5/14

The boys and the girls went a-hu-ckle-ber-ry hunting To my way - ay - ay - ay - ay - ay - ay - yah! All the boys__ and the girls went a - hu - ckle - ber - ry hunt ing to my Hi - lo my Ran - zo____ Ray

The boys and the girls went a huckleberry hunting
To my way ay, ay, ay, ay, ay, yah
All the boys and the girls went a huckleberry hunting
To my high-lo me Ranzo Ray

Oh the boys and the girls went huckleberry hunting
O the girls began to cry and the boys they stopped hunting

Then a little girl ran off and a boy he ran after
And the little girl fell down and he saw her little garter

He said "I'll be your beau if you'll have me for a feller."
But the little girl said "No, for my sweetheart's Johnny Miller."

He took her on his knee and he kissed her hard and proper
She kissed him back again and then he couldn't stop her

I'm the shantyman of the Wild Goose nation
Got a girl I left on the old plantation

Hundred Years on the Eastern Shore
(A Hundred Years Ago)

mss. no.2878 coll.20/4/14

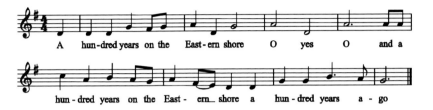

A hundred years on the Eastern shore
O yes O
A hundred years on the Eastern shore
A hundred years ago

A hundred years has passed and gone
And a hundred years will come once more

Oh Bully John from Baltimore
I knew him well on the Eastern Shore

Oh Bully John I knew him well
But now he's dead and gone to hell

A hundred years is a very long time
And a hundred years will come again

Oh don't you hear the Old Man say
One more pull and then belay

I Wish I Was With Nancy
(tune : 'I Wish I Was In Dixie')

mss. no.2905 coll.24/4/14

I wish I was with Nancy, Aye O, Aye O
In a second floor with two bob more
I'd live and die with Nancy
Aye O, Aye O, I'd live and die with Nancy

O the thing that first put my head in a flutter
Was her Balmoral boots as she cruised the gutter
Down the strand, down the strand
Down the strand, down the strand

We're outward bound from Nancy dear
Farewell you girls we'll be back next year

But when we reach Colombia's shore
With them pretty girls we'll think no more

O I wish I was in the land of cotton
Tickling up the old girls bottom

Johnnie Bowker

mss. no.2947 coll.2/6/14

Do Me Johnny Bowker
Come rock and roll me over
Do me Johnny Booker Do

Knock A Man Down (Blow the Man Down)

mss. no.2926 coll.4/5/14

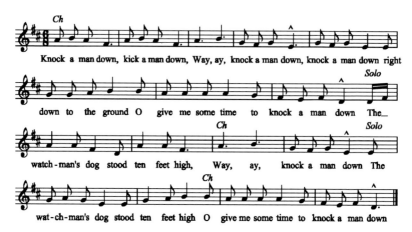

Knock a man down, kick a man down, Way, ay, knock a man down, knock a man down right
down to the ground O give me some time to knock a man down The
watch-man's dog stood ten feet high, Way, ay, knock a man down The
wat-ch-man's dog stood ten feet high O give me some time to knock a man down

Knock a man down, Kick a man down
Way ay knock a man down
Knock a man down right down to the ground
O give me some time to knock a man down

As I was a-walking down Market Street
A bully old watchman I chanced for to meet

The watchman's dog stood ten feet high
The watchman's dog stood ten feet high

I spat in his face and I gave him some jaw
Says he, me young fellow, you're breaking the law

I wish I was in London Town
It's there we'd make the girls fly round

She's a lively ship and a lively crew
O we are the boys to put her through

The rags are all gone and the chains they are jammed
The skipper he says let the weather be hanged

Liza Lee (Yankee John Stormalong)

mss. no.2956 coll.3/6/14

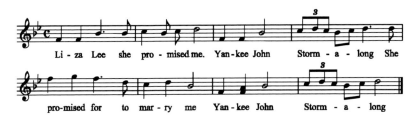

Liza Lee she promised me
Yankee John Stormalong
She promised for to marry me
Yankee John Stormalong

When I sailed across the sea
Liza said she'd be true to me

I promised her a golden ring
She promised me that little thing

Oh Liza Lee she slighted me
Now she will not marry me

Up aloft this yard must go
Mister Mate he told us so

I thought I heard the skipper say
One more pull and then belay

Lowlands (Dollar and a half a day)

mss. no.2882 coll.20/4/14

INTRO
Lowlands Lowlands hooray my John

The dollar a day is a oozier's pay
Lowlands Lowlands hooray my John
The dollar a day is a oozier's pay
The dollar and a half a day

A dollar a day is a black man's pay
Dollar and a half is a shellback's pay

What shall we poor matelos do
My dollar and a half a day

Was you ever in Mobile Bay
Screwing cotton all the day

Was you ever in Mira'shee
Where they ties up to a tree

Was you ever in I-kee-kee
Round and round the bloody bay

Was you ever in Valipo
Where the girls put on a show

I thought I heard the old man say
He would give us grog today

108

Lucy Long

mss. no.2998 coll.9/7/14

As I walked out one morning fair
To view the views& take the air
To my way-ay-ay ha ha
Me Johnny boys ha ha
Why don't you try for to wring Miss Lucy Long

There I met Miss Lucy fair
Twas there we met I do declare

I raised me hat and said hello
Hitched up and took her in tow

I wrung her all night and I wrung her all day
And I wrung her before she went away

She left me there upon the quay
Left me there and went away

Miss Lucy had a baby
She dressed it all in green

Was you ever on the Broom-a-low
Where the Yankee boys are all the go

109

Mr. Tapscott (The Irish Girl / Yellow Meal)
(tune: Larry Doonan / Can't You Dance the Polka?)

mss. no.2877 coll.20/4/14

As I was a walking down by the Clarence Dock
I overheard an Irish girl conversing with Tapscott
  And away you Santy My dear Annie
  O you Santy, I love you for your money

Good morning Mr. Tapscott, Good morning sir, said she
O have you got a ship of fame to carry me o'er the sea

O yes, I have a ship of fame, tomorrow she sets sail,
She's laying in the Waterloo Dock, A-taking in her mail

The day was fine when first we sailed but night has scarce begun
A dirty nor'west wind came up and drove us back again

Our Captain being an Irishman, as you shall understand
He hoisted out his small boat on the banks of Newfoundland

Twas at the Castle Gardens they landed me on shore
And if I marry a Yankee boy, I'll cross the seas no more

I went down to Foulton Ferry but I could not get across
I jumped on the back of a ferry-boat man and rode him like a hoss

My father is a butcher, my mother chops the meat
My sister keeps a slap up shop, a way down Water Street

Old Stormey (Mister Stormalong)

mss. no.2896 coll.22/4/14

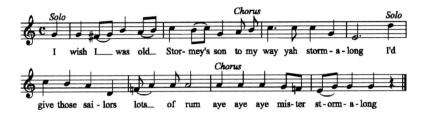

Old Stormey he is dead and gone
To my way yah Stormalong
From Cape Horn where he was born
Aye, aye, aye Mister Stormalong

Old Stormey's dead I saw him die
More than rain it dimmed my eye

And now we'll sing his funeral song
O, roll her over, long and strong

We dug his grave with a silver spade
His shroud of the finest silk was made

We lowered him down with a golden chain
And see that he don't rise again

I wish I was old Stormey's son
I'd give those sailors lots of rum

One More Day

mss. no.2883 coll.20/4/14

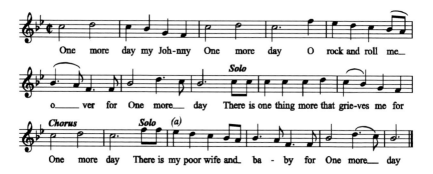

One more day my Joh-nny One more day O rock and roll me
o____ ver for One more____ day There is one thing more that grie-ves me for
One more day There is my poor wife and_ ba - by for One more____ day

SOLO INTRO / GRAND CHORUS
One more day my Johnny, one more day
O rock and roll me over for one more day

Don't you hear the Old Man roaring
    For one more day
Don't you hear the pilot bawling
    For One more day

No more gales and heavy weather
Only one more day together

I'm bound away to leave you
Don't let my parting grieve you

Can't you hear the girls a-calling
Can't you hear the capstan pawling

Put on your long-tailed blue
Your pay-days nearly due

Paddy Doyle

mss. no.2949 coll.2/6/14

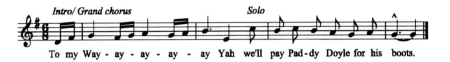

To my Way - ay - ay - ay - ay Yah we'll pay Pad-dy Doyle for his boots.

To my way ay ay ay ay yah
We'll pay Paddy Doyle for his boots

We'll order in brandy and gin

We'll all shave under the chin

The dirty old man on the poop

We'll all throw shit at the cook

Paddy Works on the Railway

mss. no.2894 coll.21/4/14

In 1841, my corduroy breeches I put on
With a stick in my fist about two feet long
To work upon the railway, the railway
I'm wearied of the railway
O poor Paddy works on the railway

In 1842, I thought this life would never do
And I resolved to put her through
A working on the railway

In 1843, I paid my passage across the sea
To New York and Amerikee
A working on the railway

In 1844, I landed on the American shore
And never to return no more
A working on the railway

In 1845 Things looked pretty well alive
And I thought to myself I would strive
A working on the railway

In 1846, When I was in a terrible fix
I thought to myself I'd take my sticks
A working on the railway

Poor Old Man (Johnny Come To Hilo)

mss. no.2880 coll.20/4/14

O a poor old man came a-riding by says I old man your horse will die
O Johnny come to Ilo, O poor old man

O wake her, O shake her,
O shake that girl with the blue dress on
O Johnny come to Ilo, Poor Old Man

And after years of sore abuse, we'll salt him down for sailors use

We'll hoist him up to the mainyard high and wish you all a long goodbye

Growl you may but go you must: growl too much your head they'll bust

Round Cape horn in frost and snow. Round Cape Horn we all must go

When we get up to Hilo town, we'll make those flash girls dance around

O a poor old man came a-riding by says I old man your horse will die

Ranzo (Poor Old Reuben Ranzo)

mss. no.2881 coll.20/4/14

INTRO
Rando boys Rando

O Ranzo was no sailor
Rando boys Rando
He shipped on board a whaler
Rando boys rando

He shipped with Captain Taylor
The man that shot the sailor

He could not do his duty
He could not boil the coffee

The Captain being a good man
He taught him navigation

We took him to the gratings
And gave him nine and thirty

O that was the end of Ranzo.
O poor old Reuben Ranzo

Rio Grande

mss. no.2907 coll.24/4/14

SOLO INTRODUCTION
O you Rio, O you Rio,
Fare you well my bonny young girls
We're bound for the Rio Grande

VERSE
O Rio Grande is my native land
  O you Rio
It's there that I would take my stand
  We're bound for the Rio Grand

GRAND CHORUS
  And away for Rio, O you Rio,
  Fare you well my bonny young girls
  We're bound for the Rio Grand

Rio Grande is the place for me
I'll pack me bags and go to sea

I wish I was in Rio today
So pack up your donkey and get under way

Bucko sailors you'll see there
With long sea-boats and close cropped hair.

In Rio Grande I want to be
It's there my Sally waits for me

She's a buxom young maid with a rolling black eye
She came from her dwelling a long way from here

I think I heard the old man say
Heave her round and then belay

Roll And Go (Sally Brown)

mss. no.2957 coll.3/6/14

INTRODUCTION
Way, ay, ay, roll and go
O Sally Brown, O Sally Brown

CHORUS
A Long Time Ago

VERSE & CHORUS
She promised for to marry me
Way, ay, ay, roll and go
O she promised for to marry me
A long time ago

O Sally Brown is the girl for me
O Sally Brown has slighted me

As I walked out one morning fair
It's there I met her I do declare

I asked her for to marry me
Marry mc or let me be

Spend me pay around the town
Left me broke and bent and down

I'll pack me bags and go to sea
And leave me Sally on the quay

119

Rosabella (Saucy Rosabella)

mss. no.2925 coll.4/5/14

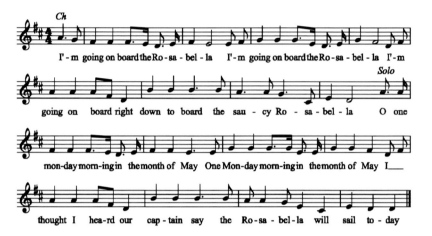

O one Monday morning in the month of May
One Monday morning in the month of May
I thought I heard our captain say
The Rosabella will sail today

I'm going on board the Rosabella
I'm going on board the Rosabella
I'm going on board, right down to board
The saucy Rosabella

Oh the Rosabella is a packet ship,
A packet ship of great reknown
And if you've heard the old refrain,
It's the song sung all a-round the town

She's a deep-water ship with a deep-water crew
She'a a deep-water ship with a deep-water crew
You can keep to the coast, but we're damned if we do
On board the Rosabella

Now the Rosabella beat the Cuyanoda,
And the Cuyanoda, beat the old Conductor
And the Boston Times says she beat them all
Sailin' out from the old North River.

Oh Black Maria is no good for me
For two years pay she took from me
She shipped me off to go to sea
On board the Rosabella

Them Ann Street gals do make me grieve
Them Ann Street gals do make me grieve
They spent me pay and made me leave
On board the Rosabella

Round the Corner Sally

mss. no.2961 coll.4/6/14

O a - round the cor - ner we will go. Round the cor - ner Sal - ly O a - round the cor - ner we__ will go. Round the cor - ner Sal - ly

Around the corner we will go
Around the corner, Sally,
Around the corner we will go
Around the corner, Sally,

Oh mademoiselle we'll take in tow
We'll take her in tow for Callao

I wish I was in Madame Gashee's
It's there me boys we'll take our ease

Around the corner we will go
To Callao through ice and snow

To Madame Gashee's we're bound to go
And mademoiselle you all do know

Haul me boys and round her up
I think me boys we've hauled enough

Rowler Bowler

mss. no.2935 coll.6/5/14

Hoo - ray you rol - ler bow- ler to my hi rig a jig and a ha, ha good morn - ing lad - ies all. O the first time that I saw her hoo - ray you rol - ler bow-ler O the first time that I saw her tw - as down in play -house square to my hi rig a jig and a ha, ha, good morn - ing lad - ies all

INTRO
Hooray you Roller Bowler
To my hi rig a jig and a ha ha
Good morning ladies all

VERSE & CHORUS
O the first time that I saw her
Hooray you roller bowler
O the first time that I saw her
'Twas down in Playhouse Square
To my hi rig a jig and a ha ha
Good morning ladies all

As I walked out one morning
Down by the riverside

She winked and tipped her flipper
I thought she was my gal

But when she found that I was skint
She left me standing there

O ladies short and ladies tall
I have had them all

Santy Anna (Plains of Mexico)

mss. no.2897 coll.22/4/14

Gen - ral Tay - lor gained the day hoo raw San - ty An - na

San - ty An - na run_ a - way All_ on the_plains of Mex - i - co

General Taylor gained the day
Hoo roo Santy Anna
Santy Anna run away
All on the plains of Mexico

O Mexico you all do know
Mexico is where I belong

O Santy Anna fought for fame
Santy Anna made his name

O Santy Anna'a dead and gone
All the fighting has been done

The Americans will make old Huerta fly
Fly away at the break of day

I wish I was in New York Town
It's there we'll make the girls fly round

Shallow Brown

mss. no.2959 coll.3/6/14

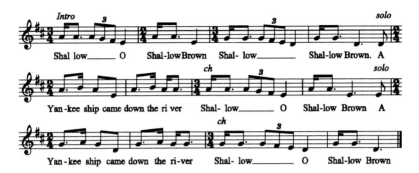

INTRO
Shallow, O Shallow Brown
Shallow, O Shallow Brown

VERSE & CHORUS
Yankee ship came down the river
Shallow, O Shallow Brown
Yankee ship came down the river
Shallow, O Shallow Brown

How d'you know she's a Yankee clipper
By the blood & guts that flow from her scuppers

And who do you think was the master of her
Bully Semmes of the Alabama

A Yankee mate and a limejuice skipper
That's the style to make you shiver

And what do you think they had for dinner
A parrot's tail and a monkey's liver

Oh me dear, I'm bound to leave yer
Do not let this parting grieve yer

One more pull and that'll do
We're the boys to pull her through

Shanadore (Shenandoah)

mss. no.2893 coll.21/4/14

O shandore I long to hear you
Hooray you rolling river
Shanadore I can't get near you
Ha ha I'm bound away on the wild Missouri

Shandore I love your daughter
I love the place she makes her water

I'm bound away I cannot stay
I'm bound away for Mobile Bay

I'm bound away for Bristol city
Where the girls they are so pretty

Seven long years I courted Sally
Seven long years I could not gain her

I gave her gold, I gave her silver
When she rolls down her tops'ls quiver

Farewell my dear I'm bound to leave you
I'm bound away but will ne'er deceive you.

Sing Fare You Well

R.R. Terry mss.

Fare you well I wish you well, Hoo - raw_____ and fare you well._____

Fare you well till I re - turn, Hoo - raw_____ sing fare you well

Fare you well, I wish you well
Hooraw and fare you well
Fare you well till I return
Hooraw sing fare you well

Fare you well we're bound away
Bound away this very day

As I walked our one morning fair
It's there I met a lady fair

At her I winked I do declare
Black as night was her raven hair

O fare you well my bonny young gel
Fare you well, I wish you well

Up aloft this yard must go
Mr. Mate he told us so

I thought I heard the skipper say
One more pull and then belay

So Early in the Morning
(The Sailor Likes His Bottle O)

mss. no.2944 coll.2/6/14

INTRO
So early in the morning
The sailor likes his bottle O

VERSE & CHORUS
A bottle of rum and a bottle of gin
And a bottle of old Jamaica ho
So early in the morning
O the sailor likes his bottle O

A bottle of wine, a bottle of beer
A bottle of Irish Whiskey-O

A packet of shag, a packet of twist
A plug of hard tabaccy-O

A Spanish girl, an Irish girl
A sailor likes the lasses O

A Yankee girl, a 'Badian girl
A smiling young mulatto

A drinking song, a loving song,
A sailor and his shipmates O

Stormalong John

mss. no.2928 coll.5/5/14

I wished I was old Stor- my's son, To my w- ay__ ay___ Storm - a -

long John. I wished I was old Stor - my's son Ha Ha

Come a - long get a - long Stor - mey a - long John

I wished I was old Stormy's son
To my way ay Stormalong John
I wished I was old Stormy's son
Ha, ha, come along, get along
Stormy along John

If I was old Stormy's son
I'd build a ship of a thousand ton

I'd treat you well and raise your pay
And stand you drinks five times a day

I'll fill you with Jamaica Rum
And every shell back would have some

Was you ever in Quebec
Stowing timber on the deck

I wished I was in Baltimore
On the good old American shore

When we get to Liverpool Town
We'll chase then Judies round and round

O Stormalong and round we go
O Stormalong through ice and snow

Sweet Nightingale

mss. no.2922 coll.4/5/14

Sweet mai-den don't fail, I will car-ry your pail, I will car-ry it right down to your

home. I will tell you a tale of a sweet night-in - gale that sings in the

val-leys below as she sings in the val-leys be-low

My sweetheart come along, don't you hear the fond song,
The sweet notes of the nightingale flow;
You shall hear the fond tale of the sweet nightingale
As she sings in the valley below
As she sings in the valley below.

Sweet maiden don't fail, for I'll carry your pail
I will carry it right down to your home
I will tell you a tale of a sweet nightingale
That sings in those valleys below
As she sings in those valleys below

Pray leave me alone, I have hands of my own,
And along with you, sir, I'll not go
For to hear…

Pray sit yourself down with me on the ground
On the banks where the primroses grow;
You shall hear…

Now this couple agreed to be married with speed,
And away to the church they did go;
Now no more she's afraid for to walk in the shade
Or to lie in the valley below…

Times Are Hard & The Wages Low
(Leave Her, Johnny, Leave Her)

mss. no.2948 coll.2/6/14

The_ time are_hard and the wa - ges low. Leave her, John - ny leave her. O the

times are hard and the wa - ges low. It's_ time for us to leave her.

The times are hard and the wages low
Leave her Johnnie leave her
O the times are hard and the wages low
It's time for us to leave her

My old mother she wrote to me
My loving son come home from sea

I've got no money I've got no clothes
I will send you money I will send you clothes

We'll leave her when we get on dock
We'll leave her and we won't come back

O, a leaking ship and a carping crew
For two long years we've pulled her through

A dollar a day is a sailors pay
To pump all night and work all day

We pumped her all around the horn
It was pump you bastards, pump or drown

I thought I heard the Captain say
We'll go ashore when we pump her dry

O leave her Johnny while you can
O leave her Johnny like a man

131

Tom's Gone To Ilo

mss. no.2902 coll.22/4/14

My Tom is gone, what shall I do
Oo way you I-lo, o, o
My Tom is gone what shall I do
My Tom is gone to I-lo

Tom is gone to Liverpool
To Liverpool that packet school

Tom is gone to Mira'shee
Where they ties up to a tree

Tom is gone to Vallipo
When he'll come back I do not know

Tom is gone to Rye-O
Where the girls put on a show

Ilo town is in Peru
Ilo's not for me and you

I wish I was in London Town
Then to sea I'd no more roam

A bully ship and a bully crew
Tom is gone and I'll go too

Tommy's Gone Away

mss. no.2929 coll.5/5/14

Tommy's gone what shall I do
My Tommy's gone away
O Tommy's gone what shall I do
My Tommy's gone away

Tommy's gone to Liverpool
To Liverpool, that noted school

Tommy's gone to Baltimore
To dance upon that sandy floor

Tommy's gone to Mobile Bay
To screw the cotton by the day

Tommy's gone to Singapore
Tommy's gone for evermore

Tommy's gone to Boneys Airs
Where the girls have long black hair

Tommy's gone for evermore
Oh Tommy's gone for evermore

Whoop Jamboree

mss. no.2923 coll.4/5/14

Now, me lads, be of good cheer,
For the Irish land will soon draw near
In a few more days we'll sight Cape Clear
O Jenny get your oatcakes done
Whoop jamboree, whoop jamboree
O you long-tailed black man, poke it up behind
Whoop jamboree, whoop jamboree
O Jenny get your oatcake done

Now Cape Clear it is in sight
We'll be off Holyhead by tomorrow night
And we'll shape our course for the Rock light
O Jenny get your oat cake done

Now me boys we're off Holyhead
No more salt beef, no more hard bread
One man in the chains for to heave the lead
O Jenny get your oat cake done

Now me lads we're round the Rock
All hammocks lashed and chests all locked
We'll haul her into the Waterloo Dock
O Jenny get your oat cake done

Now me lads we're all in dock
We'll be off to Dan Lowrie's on the spot
And now we'll have a good roundabout
O Jenny get your oat cake done

Whisky Is My Johnny

mss. no.2906 coll.24/4/14

INTRO
Whisky Johnny
O whisky is the life of man
O whisky for my Johnny

VERSE & CHORUS
I wish I had some whisky now
O Whisky Johnny
I wish I had some whisky now
O whisky for my Johnny

Whisky gave me this red nose
Whisky made me pawn me clothes

If whisky comes so near me nose
It's up it comes and down it goes

O whisky killed my sister Sue
O whisky killed an old ship's crew

A girl for ev'ry sailor man
And whisky in an old tin can

Whisky made the old man say
One more pull and then belay

Would You Go My Way

mss. no.3058 coll.23/9/14

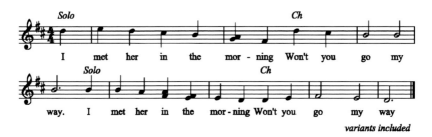

variants included

I met her in the morning
Won't you go my way
I met her in the morning
Won't you go my way

In the morning bright and early
I loved that young girl freely

She spent me money freely
She grabbed the lot – or nearly

I asked that girl to marry
She said she would rather tarry

Oh marry, never tarry (x2)

And now that I am married
I'm glad I didn't tarry

O Julia, Anna, Maria (x2)

Oh round her up so hearty
I'm jack-me-bleeding-hearty

Appendix 2: Short's Ships

This appendix gives additional information about the vessels on which John Short is known to have sailed. The vessels are listed in alphabetical order, but the chronological sequence for boats and ships on which Yankee Jack sailed is, as far as can be ascertained:

From	To	Ship	Official No.	Destination.
?	Feb 57	*Friends*	10918	Home Trade
4/2/57	12/8/57	*Promise*	23465	Cadiz, Quebec
Aut 57	22/11/57	*Cezimpra*	3982	Sicily, Malta
13/12/57	Sum.58	*Feliza*	25268	Canada
29/10/58	29/8/59	*Hugh Block*	26047	Valparaiso, Iquique
Sep 59	Aut. 60	*Earl Balcarres*	24963	Bombay, Karachi
6/10/60	15/1/62	*George Washington*	18574	Shanghai, Japan
5/2/62	5/12/62	*Woodcote*	26572	Australia
4/1/63	8/8/63	*Benjamin Buck Greene*	4683	Mauritius
19/9/63	4/5/64	*Queen of the South*	25121	Cape Town, India
9/5/64	10/9/64	*Levant*	35030	Boston
?	?	*Jane Gray*	8522	Rio
?	?	*Mary Ann*	????	New Brunswick
?	9/5/66	*Levant*	35030	Akyab (Sittwe)
9/5/66	14/1/67	*Benjamin Buck Greene*	4683	Mauritius
25/4/67	20/4/68	*Conference*	35521	Callao,Chincha Is.
1/6/68	4/9/69	*Conference*	35521	Callao, Caldera
end 69	9/6/70	*John*	22741	Home Trade
?	20/6/70	*Fortitude*	10871	Home Trade
21/6/70	30/12/70	*Charles Phillipps*	10912	Home Trade
1/1/71	30/6/72	*Hawk*	265330	Home Trade
6/8/72	19/10/72	*Telegraph*	62971	Home Trade
19/10/72	23/3/81	*Friends*	10918	Home Trade
23/3/81	21/12/81	*Crystal Bell*	62978	Home Trade
22/1/82	14/8/83	*Friends*	10918	Home Trade
Aug 83	18/3/84	*Electric*	26980	Home Trade
18/3/84	end 84	*Telegraph*	62971	Home Trade
early 85	24/4/87	*Friends*	21552	Home Trade
?	Dec 90?	*Fortitude*	10871	Home Trade
Jan 91?	? 92	*Annie Christian*	76819	Home Trade
?	late '98	*Albert*	60741	Home Trade
30/11/98	28/12/00	*Josephine Marie*	81529	Home Trade

Albert (no . 60741)

The *Albert* was a ketch. She had been built in the Channel Islands, at 56 tons and called *St. Marie*. She does not appear in the Mercantile Naval List until after 1867. In the first half of 1875 her master was Jersey-born Jacque Larbatestier – in the second half of the year James Johnson took over as master and this is, presumably, when she was sold to Luscombe, Bellamy & Co. of Plymouth. She was then registered at Plymouth, still ketch-rigged, at 46 tons. By 1883 her owner was recorded as Joseph Arthur Bellamy of 12, The Barbican, Plymouth.

By 1889, still registered at Plymouth, but her managing owner was now Alfred Nicholas of Watchet. This then remained her home port, though not her port of registry, until at least 1987 and probably through to 1903 after which she disappears from the Mercantile Naval List. John Short sailed on her immediately prior to joining *Josephine Marie* on 30th November 1898, but how long he had been on her prior to that is not known.

SOURCES:
Devon Records Office
Mercantile Naval Lists (MNL)

Annie Christian (no. 76819)

The *Annie Christian* was a vessel of which, thanks to local research, we know virtually her entire history. She was built at William Westacott's yard at Barnstaple, N. Devon, in 1881 and was single-decked, two-masted, carvel built and with an elliptic stern. A classic coasting schooner some 76.5' x 20.5' x 9' and a mere 69 tons. Her first owner, probably the man who had her built, was Edward Quayle of Ramsay, Isle of Man, where she was registered. There is no Manx record after 1883 so this is the likely date of her sale to a second owner, David B. Shaw of Wigtown, in what is now Dumfries & Galloway.

She was registered at Wigtown from 1885 to 1888 in which year she was sunk in a collision in the River Mersey. After being raised and repaired, under the ownership of the Mersey Docks & Harbour Board, her new registry and certificate of seaworthiness was issued on 12th May 1888.

Her third owner, from this point, was Isaac Allen of 7 Portland Terrace, Watchet, although she remained registered in Liverpool. It was during this period that John Short sailed on her. At the time of the 1891 census she was at Charlestown, in Cornwall, with a cargo of coal and having just survived a bad gale.

139

On a later voyage, her cargo of beans swelled and burst through her decks and, with a new deck, she was re-rigged as a ketch in November 1893 which is how her rigging remained for the rest of her life.

In July 1912 her registry in Liverpool was closed and ownership changed to the Somerset Trading Company of Bridgwater, Somerset, where she was re-registered and renamed *ADE*. By 1930 she was owned by P.W. Harris of Appledore, N. Devon, and subsequently by John Ayre of Braunton. She was eventually broken up at Appledore in 1946 – at 65 years of age.

SOURCES:
Braunton Vessels. ch.9 *in* Robert D'Arcy Andrew et al. (2007) *Braunton: Home of the last Sailing Coasters* (Braunton & District Museum, Braunton, Devon)
Crew Lists (1836 - 1901) held at the Somerset Heritage Centre.
Register Books. Merseyside Maritime Museum, Liverpool

Benjamin Buck Greene (no. 4683)

Benjamin Buck Greene was a barque of 544 tons (old style) that had been built in Cowes, Isle of Wight, in 1846 and was owned by H.D. & Jas Blythe and Greene, 15 Philpot Lane, London where she was also registered.

She made the trip to Mauritius on a regular basis certainly from 1848 to at least 1872 according to the *Lloyd's Registers*, under a series of masters: '51-'58 Miller, '58-'61 Grierson, '61-'66 Pearne, '66-'69 Overstone, '69/'70 Ovenden, '70-'72 Benwell, '72-'75 Bowman.

She underwent repairs in '59 and was re-registered at 528 tons (new style). The *Benjamin Buck Greene* underwent further repairs in '67 presumably in consequence of damage sustained on the '66/'67 trip on which John Short sailed.

SOURCES:
Lloyd's Registers (LR)
Mercantile Naval Lists (MNL)

Cezimpra (no. 3982)

Cezimpra, named after the Portuguese port of that name some 30 miles south of Lisbon, was built in Bideford, Devon, in 1853 and was registered at Bristol on 13th November 1854. At 130 tons, she was schooner-rigged, had single deck and 2 masts; 80.7 ft. long, 16.8 ft. in the beam and 16 ft. in the hold; she was owned by Fernandez, captained by R. Hocking, and worked from Bideford in the Home Trade.

In 1856 ownership transferred to J. Dyer and *Cezimpra* was re-registered in Bristol at only 89 tons – presumably following a re-fit. Under the captaincy of R. Uran she then sailed regularly to St. Michèl until, in 1859, still owned by Dyer, her registry is changed to Falmouth on 10th May. M. Radmore then took over as captain and, according to subsequent *Lloyd's Registers*, she started to undertake voyages into the Mediterranean. It was on one of these trips that John Short sailed on her - trading into Catania, on Sicily, and to Malta as part of the copper ore trade.

By 1860, ownership had again changed, now to Thomas Mitchell of Devoran and she remained registered at Falmouth. On 27th February 1860, outward bound from Swansea with a cargo of coal and running for shelter from a north-west gale, she ran aground behind the breakwater at Bude, Cornwall. Rocket lines fired from shore all missed their mark, but eventually the crew were all saved thanks to the efforts of four local men who, standing in the breakers, held taut a line that had been thrown from *Cezimpra*. The four men (Robert Hoyle, chief boatman of coastguard; Thomas Bean, seaman; William Peardon, seaman; and John Hoyle, carpenter) each received £1 from the Mercantile Marine Fund for their efforts. By 11 a.m. the following morning *Cezimpra* had become a total wreck.

SOURCES:
Lloyd's Registers (LR)
Mercantile Naval Lists (MNL)
Lloyd's List (LL)
Grahame Farr mss @ Bristol Records Office.
Larne. *Shipwreck Index of the British Isles Vol.1.*

Charles Phillipps (no. 10912)

At only 20 tons *Charles Phillips* had been built in Padstow in 1830 and it was there she was initially registered. Carvel built with a round stern, with one deck and one mast, she was rigged as a sloop. Her dimensions were 48.2' x 17.1' x 6.9' in the hold. Under a bill of sale dated 21/10/1849 ownership changed to Henry Chidgey of Watchet where she became registered on 22/5/1850 (port no. 8). Her master at Watchet was William Allen. Her certificate of registry was lost when she was stranded on 18/5/1856 and she was subsequently re-registered, at 32 tons, (port no. 7) on 1/4/1857 with Richard Dales Case as her new owner. He remained her owner until 1871 when she was transferred to Joseph Pittaway who had previously been her master. Re-registered again (port no. 11), with another change of tonnage, on 27/9/1873, she was eventually wrecked on the Rock in Porlock Bay on 14/11/1882.

SOURCES:
Crew Lists (1836 - 1901) held at the Somerset Heritage Centre.
Bridgwater Port Shipping Registers (1786 – 1906) held at the Somerset Heritage Centre.

Conference (no. 35521)

The 967-ton *Conference* was built at Richibucto, New Brunswick, Canada, in 1856 and was owned by John Power. Her first master was W. Long, and she was initially registered at Mirimichi. *Conference* had 2 decks and was a ship-rigged three-masted vessel, carvel built and with a square stern; 177.2 ft. long, 36.3 wide and 21.8 deep in the hold.

She was sold, according to a certificate of sale dated 2nd December 1856 made by Jardine & Jardine, attorneys for the then owner John Power, to a new owner, Samuel Robert Graves of Liverpool. He is recorded as her sole owner (64 shares) from 10th December 1856.

Ownership subsequently changed to Charles Hill & Sons of Bristol on 25th April 1867, and her registry was changed to that port (port no. 61). Her master then became Capt. E. J. Bolt of Appledore, Devon. *Conference* sailed regularly around the Horn to South America in the guano and mineral trades: to Callao, Caldera, Pisco and the Chincha Islands, her voyages and cargoes reflecting the change in fertiliser use from Peruvian guano to Chilean mineral nitrates. Short sailed on her for two consecutive voyages: April '67 – September '69. Her career ended when she foundered at Huanillos in Peru on 9th May 1877.

SOURCES
Lloyd's Registers (LR)
Mercantile Naval Lists (MNL)
Crew lists & Log Books held at the Bristol Records office
Grahame Farr mss @ Bristol Records Office.
Register Books. Merseyside Maritime Museum, Liverpool
http://www.pro.rcip-chin.gc.ca/bd-dl/nav-ship-eng.jsp

Crystal Bell (no. 62978)

Crystal Bell was originally built in France and called *Emile et Charles*. In June 1871 she was registered at Bridgwater (port no. 7) at 106 tons, and owned by George Passmore of Watchet. Her dimensions were 80' x 21' x 10.5' with a single deck, two masts and schooner rigged. Passmore had her refitted and re-registered at 95 tons in January 1872. She remained with the same owner from 1871 to 1882 and plied her 'home trade' voyages round the coast as far as Yarmouth and Liverpool, across to Ireland and over the channel to Antwerp and Boulogne (see appendix 4 for exemplary details of her voyages in 1880-1882). With licensed accommodation for 7 or 8, she frequently carried far less crew – for example, at the 1881 census, when she is away from her home port, she has only the Master, the Mate and the cook. During 1880 the master of the vessel changes from William Escott to William Organ.

She was mortgaged on several occasions and in 1881, following a writ *fieri facias* against George Passmore for debt, she was confiscated by the High Sheriff of Monmouth and sold on to Richard Coomes of Teignmouth whence her registry was changed in March 1882. William Organ remained, at least initially, as the Master. In January 1884, on a voyage from Runcorn to Plymouth, she foundered and was lost, although all the crew were saved.

SOURCES:
Crew Lists (1836 - 1901) held at the Somerset Heritage Centre.
Bridgwater Port Shipping Registers (1786 – 1906) held at the Somerset Heritage Centre.

Earl Balcarres (no. **24963***)*

The East Indiaman *Earl Balcarres* was designed and built by Wadia at Bombay for the East India Company, and named in honour of the 6th Earl Balcarres - Alexander Lindsay (1752-1825). She was built of teak and was the supreme example of the old type of Indiaman: she had two tiers of guns making her look more like a man-o-war than a merchantman. She measured 139 feet in length with a 44 foot beam and displaced 1417 tons. Launched on the 25th March 1811, she was fitted for sea by 1815. Her E.I.C. identity number was 932 and she completed nine voyages for the Company between 1815 and 1833 after which, together with *Thomas Coutts*, *Abercrombie Robinson*, *Lowther Castle*, *George the Fourth*, *JAVA* and the rest of the E.I.C. fleet, she was sold as a consequence of the Act of August 1833 which required the company to dispose of its assets.

For five years she was captained by James Jameson and, in 1821, he passed command to Peter Cameron. She ran the tea route into China, calling at Calcutta although this would be changed to Bombay in her later years with the Company. Her last two voyages for the Company commenced in April 1830 and May 1832 and were direct to China – when she returned from the last trip, on 25th May 1833, she was moored in the Thames until purchased by Thomas Shuter for £10,709 in September 1834. Under his ownership, she still traded into India and the Far East but in 1838 she was sold to Somes Bros. of London.

Joseph Somes (1787-1845) had been born in Stepney, London. He took over the family business in 1816 and, under his guidance, it became the largest ship-owner in England. Somes was a strong advocate of the *Lloyd's Register of Shipping* which started in 1764. He also invested his wealth in colonial companies, and was famous for chartering vessels to the government – for the movement of troops, the transport of convicts and the supply of outposts in Australia. Somes became Governor of New Zealand in 1840 and also became a Member of Parliament, representing the constituency of Dartmouth from 27th December 1844 until he died just over six months later. Towards the end of his life, he was partnered by his sons and by the time of his death, Somes Bros. had become 'The Merchant Shipping Company'.

From 1848 the *Earl Balcarres* continued to operate, mostly in the India trade, until she was no longer fit for long voyages. Up to 1855 she was captained by Morice, then by Bremmer. Morice (or Morris) returned for one trip in '60/'61, before Stephen captained her until she was sold. In May 1863, ownership passed to the African Steam Ship Company who used her as a hulk on the west coast of Africa, off Sierra Leone, conceivably as a holding vessel for the slave trade. Although Lincoln's Emancipation Proclamation against slavery was made in 1863, the 13th Amendment of the Constitution, which finally abolished slavery and involuntary servitude in the U.S.A., was only passed by Congress in January 1865 and ratified in December of that year. *Earl Balcarres* remained off Sierra Leone for eight years until finally broken up in 1875.

SOURCES:
Lloyd's Registers (LR)
Mercantile Naval Lists (MNL)
Lloyd's List (LL)
www.archives.gov/historical-docs/document.html

Electric (no 62980)
Electric had been built at Westacott's yard in Barnstaple, Devon in 1871. Carvel built, with an elliptical stern, she had a single deck and single mast which was smack-rigged. *Electric* was 64' x 19.6' x 7.9' and was registered as 45 tons.

She was registered at Bridgwater on 27th Sept.1871. William Stoate was initially her owner and shares passed within the family, to James Stoate and to William jnr. These two are the owners after William snr. died in December1890. The Stoate family owned several ships at Watchet including *Hawk* and *Telegraph* (see below). John Nicholas was master in 1884, and Joseph Pittaway from 1893. *Electric* was eventually wrecked at Watchet in September 1903 and the registry was closed later that month.

SOURCES:
Crew Lists (1836 - 1901) held at the Somerset Heritage Centre.
Bridgwater Port Shipping Registers (1786 – 1906) held at the Somerset Heritage Centre.

Feliza (no. 25269)

Feliza was a ship-rigged three-master although only 324 tons burthen. Built in Bristol in 1820, she had 2 decks and was 103.6 ft. long, 26.6 ft wide and was 5.9 ft. tween-decks. In Pigot's Directory of Gloucester for 1930 she is listed as voyaging from Bristol to Jamaica, mastered by F. Cundy, one of three master mariners of the surname Cundy sailing out of Bristol.

Michael Bouquet lists her as a Barque and she may well have been adapted from her original ship-rig conformation. *Lloyd's Register* gives her as owned, from (at least) 1850/'51 to 1852/'53, by Miles & Co. of Bristol and mastered by T. Smith. During this period she sailed regularly from Bristol to the West Indies. In '53/'54 she is not listed but in '54/'55 ownership has changed to Perrin & Co. and the master is now Thomas Vincent. In this period she sailed from Bristol to the Cape of Good Hope. She was eventually lost in the North Sea, after a forty-year career, in October 1860.

SOURCES:
Lloyd's Registers (LR)
Mercantile Naval Lists (MNL)
Lloyd's List (LL)
Grahame Farr mss @ Bristol Records Office
Pigot's Directory of Gloucestershire, 1830

Fortitude (no. 10871)

Fortitude was 'foreign-built' in 1815 and first registered at Bridgwater (port no. 12) in 1837. She was re-registered (port no. 9) in September 1864 with her owner recorded as Richard Wedlock (this is likely to be an error for Wedlake). At just over 40 tons, she was sloop rigged and had a single deck and single mast. Both Richard and Mary Wedlock [*sic*] had equal shares. At the end of September 1870 ownership changed to John Allen, and then to Mary Allen in March 1884. Mary twice mortgaged her to John Hawkes Allen – the second mortgage being discharged on 1st January 1890. *Fortitude* was eventually broken up in June 1893 and the registry closed on 14th July that year.

SOURCES:
Crew Lists (1836 - 1901) held at the Somerset Heritage Centre.
Bridgwater Port Shipping Registers (1786 – 1906) held at the Somerset Heritage Centre.

Friends (no. 10918)

One of five vessels named *Friends* which were registered at Bridgwater! This boat was built in Watchet and originally registered there in April 1852 and her tonnage is given in the Port Shipping Register as 87.74. She was carvel-built with a square stern, a single deck and two masts. Her dimensions were 55.7' x 17.1' x 7.1'.

Her owner from 1867-1871 was George Pole. Ownership then changed to Llewellyn Hole in 1872 and she was re-registered at Bridgwater in November 1872 (port no. 4) at 31 tons. Hole remained her owner through to 1896. John Short's father, Richard, was Master of *Friends* from December 1851 through to May 1872. The registers note that Richard Short had 'no certificate' i.e. no Masters ticket. The seaman's 'ticket' system was only introduced in 1845 – many seamen who had sailed previously did not bother with a ticket: experience, particularly in the Home Trade, was regarded as of greater value!

Friends met a sorry end when she was wrecked in Watchet harbour in the storm of the night of 28th December 1900. See also *Josephine Marie*.

SOURCES:
Crew Lists (1836 - 1901) held at the Somerset Heritage Centre
Bridgwater Port Shipping Registers (1786 – 1906) held at the Somerset Heritage Centre

Friends (no. 21552)

This *Friends* had been built at Appledore, N. Devon, in 1818, so she was by no means young when George Green, as owner, first registered her at Bridgwater (port no. 11) on 13th September 1853. She was a 49 ton coastal vessel, rigged as a dandy. *Friends* was 56' long, 17' in the beam and with a hold depth of 8.4'. Shares were divided between George Green, John Ridler and John Thorne in March 1857. By November 1973 she was wholly owned by John Thorne.

Her master was Thomas Martin Davis until 1870 when William Escott took over. Thomas Redd (or, more likely, Ridd) was her master on the 1871 returns and he remained through to 1886. In 1887-'89 her master was now William Norman, who is listed as both Owner and Master by 1891. She is missing from crew lists in 1892 and 1893, but in 1894 she reappears still with Thorne as owner and with her master now recorded as Vickery. 1895 is also missing, and in 1886 William and Francis Norman are listed as Owners, with John Binding as Master.

John Thorne remained her owner until he sold her to William Norman on 8th May 1901, and a mere 16 days later, on the 24th, she foundered off the Nore Point and was lost.

SOURCES:
Crew Lists (1836 - 1901) held at the Somerset Heritage Centre
Bridgwater Port Shipping Registers (1786 – 1906) held at the Somerset Heritage Centre

George Washington (no. 18574)

A 414-ton clipper ship built and registered at Aberdeen by Thomas Wright. Her keel was laid in 1856 and she was launched in March 1857. Carvel built, with a single deck and a round stern, she had three masts and was barque-rigged with a male figurehead. At 149.9 ft. long, she had a beam of 27.3 ft. and a depth of 16.5 ft.

Her master, while she was owned by Wright, was J. Joss but, only three months after being launched, in June 1857, she was sold to William Escombe of the Escombe Bros. from London. Joss sailed her from Aberdeen to London and her new owners.

There she was fitted with felt and yellow metal, retained her barque rig, and was re-registered in London. Initially mastered by Copeland, she was taken over by William Dempster in 1860. The *Aberdeen Journal* of 19th December 1860 reported that on 12th November, the ship had been at 8N, 23.40W, that is mid-Atlantic between West Africa and Brazil, on a voyage from London to Shanghai. In the same issue was given a notice that 33/64th shares in *George Washington* were for sale. Whether the shares were bought up is unclear, but William Escombe remained the managing owner. On this voyage in 1860/'61 she evidently suffered damage, as repairs were carried out before her next voyage which was to Algoa Bay. Given the destination, it is likely that this '60/'61 voyage was the one on which Short sailed.

In 1863, still owned by the Escombe brothers, L. Jack took over as Master In August 1865 ownership transferred to the Liverpool merchants Peter Stuart and Peter Douglas, with equal shares, but by 1870 she was owned by George Drover jnr. of Cowes, on the Isle of Wight.

Eventually, at the furthest point of a voyage to China, the *George Washington* was left in the possession of the British Consul in Shanghai. She had caught fire and subsequently had been condemned. Her 'Form 20' was received on 10th December 1875 and her registry was closed on 19th January 1876.

SOURCES:
Lloyd's Registers (LR)
Mercantile Naval Lists (MNL)
Lloyd's List (LL)
Aberdeen Register of Shipping (Aberdeen City Archives).
Register Books. Merseyside Maritime Museum, Liverpool
www.aberdeenships.com

Hawk (no. 265330)

Hawk had been built at Southtown in Suffolk in 1846, and was registered at
Bridgwater (port no. 2) on 9th January 1867, having been bought by William
Prosser and Charles Williams. *Hawk* was 76 tons, a carvel built two-mast
schooner. In June 1883, Prosser's shares transferred to Williams who immediately
sold the vessel on to John Moses of Newport, Monmouth, to whence her registry
was changed.

In January 1865 she was bought by William Stoate and brought back to
Bridgwater to join his family's various vessels (see also *Electric* and *Telegraph*):
she was re-registered (port no. 2) in January 1865. Re-registered again at the same
port (port no. 8) on 30th August 1870, she was only 59 tons. Owned from '69 –
'72 by William Stoate, her masters were: Alfred Wedlake ('69) and Robert
Wedlake ('70-72).

In February 1885 she was stranded near Cherbourg but evidently not lost as she
appears re-registered yet again, and still owned by William Stoate, at Bridgwater
(port no. 8) in 1910.

SOURCES:
Crew Lists (1836 - 1901) held at the Somerset Heritage Centre
Bridgwater Port Shipping Registers (1786 – 1906) held at the Somerset Heritage Centre

Hugh Block (no. 26047)

The *Hugh Block* was a 232-ton barque or brig of Southampton. She had been built
in 1823 and was owned by John Ransom of Southampton through until 1868 after
which she is no longer listed. The master until 1857 was J. Abbatt and she seems
only to have sailed between Southampton and Liverpool. In 1857 Chapman took
over as master and her voyages are no clearer. However when John Short sailed
on her in the late '50s or early '60s it was to Iquique and Valparaiso on the West
coast of South America, and in all probability she did so throughout her life.
Chapman remained her master through to 1866 when her voyages are clearly
defined as being Southampton to South America. In 1866 Helyer took over as

148

master and her voyages to South America continued. She disappears from the listings after 1868.

The owner, John Ransom (1799-1886), served his apprenticeship with a local shipbuilder before setting up on his own, at Belvidere Yard, Crosshouse, Southampton. He was a prominent local ship-owner and shipbuilder with a fleet of over 20 vessels. *Mary Block* was another of his vessels. He died in 1886 and, in his will, left his yard to James Dible and his two sons (J. Dible and Sons), along with his remaining vessels: *Fortunate* (no. 13923 – 1849), *Charles Napier* (no. 24216 - 1854), *Crosshouse* (no. 51289 – 1865), *Hannah Ransom*,(no. 62222 - 1870), *Primrose* (no. not traced) and *Fonthill* (no. 76843 - 1878).

SOURCES:
Lloyd's Registers (LR)
Mercantile Naval Lists (MNL)
Lloyd's List (LL)
www.diaperheritage.com/exhibition/at_sea/index.php
www.nationalarchives.gov.uk/a2a/records.aspx?cat=043-clasa&cid=-1#-1

Jane Gray (no. 8522)

The *Jane Gray* was a barque of 287 tons built in Sunderland in 1852 and registered at Newcastle. She obviously had problems for she underwent repairs in 1854 under the ownership of G. Gray. Her master was P. Pinet. She needed further repairs in 1856 and was then captained by John Wherry of Glasgow until October 1862. During this time her ownership apparently changed from G. Gray to J. Gray. This may be a formal transfer or inheritance from husband to wife if, as may be assumed, the J. Gray to whom ownership apparently transfers was a wife after whom the ship was originally named. During this time she sailed regularly to Australia.

Further repairs were needed in 1862 and she was clad in felt and yellow metal. On the 9th October 1862 her registry changed from Newcastle to London, and her ownership likewise from J. Gray to Adamson. She was now captained by Alexander Chalmers. There are no crewlists for Oct. '63 to Oct. '64, but on that date she commenced a voyage which would take her to Malaga and then Cadiz, where Chalmers was discharged 'by order of the owners', for reasons unspecified, and replaced by John Wherry, who had been her Captain previously. It may just be that Chalmers was a temporary Captain pending the planned return of Wherry. The vessel sailed from Cadiz on 9th January 1864 for the West Indies and the USA. She then went on to Uruguay: arriving at Paysandú on 28th April, at Fray Bentos on 25th May and at Montevideo on 4th July where she remained for three days. From thence she sailed home, where the voyage ended on the 10th September 1864.

Voyage details are again missing from the records between September 1864 and January 1866. In February 1866 *Jane Gray* has her registry changed from London to Shields and she was then owned by John Dixon of Blythe. Thereafter, with complete voyage records available, it is shown that under a series of Captains (George Davis, William Lake and James Hill) she sailed regularly between Blythe and the French Channel ports, even venturing to Spain and the Mediterranean, although most frequently into the Baltic: Riga, Gulf of Finland, Kattegat, Cronstadt and Bothnia, almost certainly in the timber trade.

Between a voyage ending in October 1869 and another starting in April 1870 ownership of *Jane Gray* transferred to Robert Cubitt-Wells of Blakeney, Norfork. Henry Pinchen of Clay, Norfolk, now became her master. This partnership remained, with *Jane Gray* sailing regularly in the timber trade between the North East, London, Rotterdam and into the Baltic and, from 1872 onwards, into the Mediterranean until 1874, after which there is no record of her.

SOURCES:
Lloyd's Registers (LR)
Mercantile Naval Lists (MNL)
Crew Lists, Agreements, etc. held in the Maritime History Research Collection, University of Newfoundland, St John's, Newfoundland,

John (no. 22741)
The *John* was built at Milford in 1846. A carvel-built, 76-ton, two-masted schooner, she was 53ft. long and just over 14 ft. in the beam.

Registered at Bridgwater (port no. 4), at 42 tons, on 4th October 1869, she was now owned by Joseph Lewis Kingsbury but ownership transferred to William Johnson in 1870 and he remained her owner until she was wrecked, in July 1873, between Slade and the Hook Light, Co. Waterford.

SOURCES:
Crew Lists (1836 - 1901) held at the Somerset Heritage Centre
Bridgwater Port Shipping Registers (1786 – 1906) held at the Somerset Heritage Centre

Josephine Marie (no. 81529)
94-ton gross (78 nett.), *Josephine Marie* was a two-mast schooner built in Nantes in 1861. She was carvel-built with a square stern, 70 ft. long, 21.6 ft. in the beam

and with a hold depth of nearly 10'. She was first registered at Bridgwater (port no. 2) in April 1882 when she was jointly owned by William and John Besley. She remained in the ownership of the Belsley family until she was destroyed, on 28th December 1900, when a massive gale breached the harbour at Watchet. The *Josephine Marie* broke her moorings and smashed into the schooner *Hermatite,* both ships becoming write-offs. Altogether five ships were destroyed as well as the harbour itself.

SOURCES:
Michael Bouquet's notebooks
Crew Lists (1836 - 1901) held at the Somerset Heritage Centre
Bridgwater Port Shipping Registers (1786 – 1906) held at the Somerset Heritage Centre

Levant (no. 35030)
The *Levant* was a North American ship of 1436 tons, built in St. John's in 1841 by Francis, Joseph and Thomas D. Ruddock. She was registered as owned equally by them at New Brunswick (port no.16). She was 186 ft. long, 38.2 in the beam and 22.35 deep. On 1st May 1856 the attorney for the Ruddocks, William J. Lamport, issued a certificate of sale, for effect from 27th August of that year, in favour of Twist Thomas Keynon, Charles Wilson and the Rathbones (Samuel Grey, William Snr. and Willian Jnr.), all of Liverpool. The Canadian registry was closed on the 18th October 1856 and registry transferred to Liverpool (port no. 262). This transfer year has sometimes been erroneously quoted as the year in which she was built.

Several writers about Short's life, quoting earlier writers, claim that the *Levant*, along with some two hundred or so other Northern (Union) vessels, changed registry to Liverpool in order to avoid interception by Southern States (Confederacy) vessels during the American Civil War but, as quoted above, the *Levant* had been registered in Liverpool since the end of 1856, over four years before the start of the American Civil War – in any case, her earlier registry had been Canadian! Her Liverpool registry gives her as a 1210-ton vessel clad with felt and yellow metal. Undoubtedly many vessels did change from U.S. registry to U.K. in order to avoid Southern raiders such as the *CSS Alabama* – but *Levant* was not one of them. Notwithstanding, she was frequently listed as an 'American ship' even when her registry was firmly in Liverpool. The reasons are elusive: she even only had three Northern Americans in her crew at the time Short sailed on her – and two of them were Canadian.

She was registered as owned by the same merchants, led by the Rathbones, from her 1856 purchase right through until 1870 when she was sold to George Dryden of N. Shields. From 1858, and probably from 1856, her master was Cpt. Fearan until, in 1865, D. Ross took over as Master. Ross remained as Captain until the *Levant* was sold on to Dryden.

Dryden did not own her for long, as she was finally lost when she foundered, in October 1871, near Outer Dowsing – a shoal off Gibraltar Point, Lincolnshire, at the North 'corner' of The Wash. Her certificate of registry was lost with the vessel and her registration was finally closed on 27th October, her Form 20 being received on the 30th.

SOURCES:
Lloyd's Registers (LR)
Mercantile Naval Lists (MNL)
Lloyd's List (LL)
Register Books. Merseyside Maritime Museum, Liverpool
Canadian Public Archives: RG 42 Vol.1350. (original references: vol.139, Reel C,-387
     p.83)
Crew Lists, Agreements, Maritime History Research Collection, University of Newfoundland
www.pro.rcip-chin.gc.ca/bd-dl/nav-ship-eng.jsp

Mary Ann (no. 48207)
There are 296 boats named *Mary Ann* in the St. John's Canadian registry (and another 6 named *Mary Anne*). We do not have solid evidence from Short's papers as to exactly which ship she was, nor which master or owner he served under. Michael Bouquet is certain that the *Mary Ann* on which John Short told him that he had sailed to New Brunswick to load timber was the one whose official number was 48207.

Built in New Brunswick in 1863, at 427 tons, this *Mary Ann* was a ship of St. John and was initially owned by William Maynes of Rothsay, King's County, New Brunswick. She does not appear in MNL, LR or the Canadian registry until 1867 when, according to MNL, she is owned by W.M. McLean of St. John. From 1867 until 1874 she appears in LR as owned by McLean, mastered by Delaney, and voyaging regularly between St. John and Caernarvon. LR however, is incorrect – over several years.

According to the Ship Information Database of the Canadian Heritage Information Network (C.H.I.N.), this *Mary Ann* only ever made two voyages. The first departed St. John on 17th March 1864, sailing to Havana, Trinidad and Greenock, returning to St. John on 23rd October.

The second voyage, over a year later, started from St. John on 23rd August 1866 sailing to Liverpool. She left Liverpool with Cuba as her destination, making the Irish coast on 10th December where she was 'wrecked off Cape Clear' following two gales. The relevant LL entry is quoted in the text of this book. C.H.I.N. then shows the Canadian registry as being closed and 'sent to London' 1 January 1867.

SOURCES:
Lloyd's Registers (LR)
Mercantile Naval Lists (MNL)
Lloyd's List (LL)
www.pro.rcip-chin.gc.ca/bd-dl/nav-ship-eng.jsp

Promise (no. 23465)

Promise was the first vessel on which John Short went deep-sea. He sailed on her shortly before he turned 18, in 1857. Variously reported as a barque of London or as a brig of Bristol, she was in fact a London-registered vessel which had been built in Sunderland in 1845. She sailed regularly from the Severn Estuary (Cardiff and Bridgwater), and occasionally London, to Quebec, frequently calling at Cadiz or Gibraltar en route. *Promise* appears in MNL ('57- '64) but not LR for those years. In MNL '66 she has changed ownership to James Terry of Whitby, although Terry appears to have been her master, certainly from 1856 onwards. From around 1859 she appears to have given up the trans-Atlantic trade and simply ran up and down the East coast of England to the West coast of Spain and Gibraltar. In 1866 she was re-registered at Whitby at 396 tons. There are no entries in 1867 or thereafter.

SOURCES:
Lloyd's Registers (LR)
Mercantile Naval Lists (MNL)
Lloyd's List (LL)

Queen of the South (no. 25121)

Queen of the South was different to every other vessel on which John Short sailed – she had a steam engine. She was a full-rigged ship of 1433 tons but also carried an 300 horse-power auxiliary engine which would keep her under way, at up to 10 knots, if the wind failed. Such hybrid ships were, for a couple of decades, regarded as the best of both worlds: iron hulls and far bigger engines would displace sail altogether in the end. Built in 1852 by C.J. Mare & Co. of Blackwall, London for James Laming's General Screw Steam Shipping Co., she was the first of six sister ships each with an 800 horse-power engine: *Lady Jocelyn* (no. 11923 of 1650 tons), *Indiana* (no. 13849 of 1798 tons), *Calcutta* (no. 7887 of 1664 tons),

Mauritius (no. 26216 of 1451 tons) and *Hydaspes* (no. 25134 of 1236 tons) which serviced the monthly mail contracts that had been won between Plymouth and Cape Horn (1850), to Australia (in 1852) and to India (Calcutta and Madras) and calling at the isles of St. Vincent, Ascension and St. Helena, as well as at Cape Town, Mauritius and Ceylon (also 1852).

All ships in the GSSS Co. fleet were chartered to the government for army transport during the Crimean War in 1854-1855 and, in 1856, official papers show that in January 'This vessel has been given up by the Government.' However, in February, 'The General Screw Co. have received an intimation that the government might require the use of their 4 large ships now lying in Southampton Docks – viz. – the *Calcutta*, *Argo*, *Hydaspes* and *Queen on the South*, for transport service.' She *was* required! At Balaclava, in 1856, the '*Queen of the South* arrived from Malta on 18th November with quantities of warm clothing' for the troops and a report of 22nd November stated that 'Yesterday the "*Queen of the South*" disembarked draughts of Guards to the amount of 800 men.' British troop involvement in the Crimea did not immediately end with the Crimea War itself in February 1856.

In 1857, following peace in the Crimea, the entire GSSS Co. fleet was sold, and ownership of the *Queen of the South* passed to the European & American Steam Shipping Company (1857-1859). The new company was managed by T.R. Croskey who was the American Consul at Southampton. Croskey & Co. were also agents for the American-owned Ocean Steam Navigation Company (OSNC), which was running a monthly service between New York, Southampton and Bremen. The *Queen of the South* and the *Croesus* (another OSNC steamer) each sailed once a month on this service on alternate dates with American Steamers, thereby providing a combined weekly sailing from Southampton. In early 1857 the United States Postmaster General awarded the contract to carry mails from New York to a more modern fleet and the Ocean Steam Navigation Company ceased trading in July 1857 although, due to a lack of buyers, the fleet was not sold until 1858.

In 1859 the *Queen of the South* was re-sold, this time to the Anglo Luso Brazilian Royal Mail Steam Navigation Company of Portugal and was renamed *The Milford Haven* but in 1861 she was sold again, to the East India & London Shipping Co., and her original name, *Queen of the South,* was restored.

By 1862 she was again in use as a troop carrier: one voyage to Madras, Calcutta and Cape Town lasted from 15th October 1862 to 1st June 1863, under the captaincy of William Thornhill, and this was followed by another voyage to the same ports from September 1863 to May 1864, under the captaincy of William

Stewart. This was the trip on which both John Short and his younger brother Sydney sailed, at the end of which she collided with and sank *Crescent* of Swansea. *Queen of the South* was subsequently used by the EI&LS Co. in the emigrant trade to Australia, one example from the press reporting that having left Liverpool on the 31st July 1865, she arrived at Hobart on 31st October (92 days) with 434 emigrants. There had been thirteen deaths and four births on board during the voyage.

Queen of the South continued her Australia runs until 1871 when she was again sold and, with the engine removed, converted into a purely sailing ship, and renamed *Malta*. On 24th November 1885 *Malta* was wrecked near Sandy Hook, New Jersey – the end of an extensive and diverse career.

SOURCES:
Lloyd's Registers (LR)
Mercantile Naval Lists (MNL)
Illustrated London News – Feb 4 – 1865
Crew Lists & Log Books (Oct 1862 – May 1864) held @ University of Newfoundland
www.pbenyon.plus.com/18-1900/P/03752.html
www.crimeantexts.org.uk/sources/reports/mntrept2.html
www.historic-shipping.co.uk

Telegraph (no. 62971)

The *Telegraph* was built at Westacott's yard in Barnstaple, N. Devon for William Stoate and immediately registered at Bridgwater (port no.6) on 22nd November 1869. She was carvel-built with a round stern, 61 ft. x 19.1 ft. x 7.7 ft. Initially rigged as a smack with a single mast, she was converted, within a month, to a two-mast dandy, and re-registered. She weighed 40.85 tons. Rather like *Electric* and *Hawk*, which were also owned by the Stoates, share ownership passed among William and his two sons:

On 30th April 1880, Wm. Stoate owns $^{32}/_{64}$, John Stoate $^{16}/_{64}$ and Wm. Stoate jnr. $^{16}/_{64}$.

On 6th September 1887, Wm. snr. is still registered as owner, but the shares are redistributed with James Stoate $^{21}/_{64}$, John $^{22}/_{64}$, and Wm. jnr. $^{21}/_{64}$.

On 12th May1891, James and Wm. jnr. retain the same, but the 21 shares previously owned by John are transferred, on his death to his executors jointly: to Wm. Cole, Sarah Jane Stoate and James Henson.

At a later date still, James and Wm. jnr. alone own the boat with $^{32}/_{64}$ shares each.

She had a series of Masters: John Wedlake (1869-76), George Wedlake (1876-1885), Wilkins (1886), Joseph Pittaway (1887), Robert Nicholas (1893-1896).

In February 1912, James and William jnr. sold *Telegraph* to Walter John Webber who, in March 1918 sold her again, to Thomas Watts of Braunton at which time the registry was transferred to Barnstaple.

SOURCES:
Crew Lists (1836 - 1901) held at the Somerset Heritage Centre
Bridgwater Port Shipping Registers (1786 – 1906) held at the Somerset Heritage Centre
Ben Norman. *Tales of Watchet Harbour* (see Bibliography)

Woodcote (no. 26572)
The *Woodcote* of Swansea was 474 tons. With a length of 154.4 ft., breadth of 26.14 ft., and depth of 17.5 ft., she had been built at Shields in 1855 although she was registered at London throughout her career. She was involved in the emigrant trade to the Antipodes in the late '50s and early '60s, and her voyages included Ceylon (Sri Lanka) and the Indian sub-continent in the mid-'60s. Initially owned by George Marshall and captained by John (or Henry) Fleming, ownership transferred to Thomas Eldridge in 1858 although Fleming stayed as master. This ownership and captaincy remained until 1868 when F. Wilson took over as captain. The *Woodcote* was initially clad in yellow metal in 1855 and then with the addition of felt from 1860.

The repair and re-cladding in 1860 was consequent upon the *Woodcote* becoming stranded in the English Channel. She ran onto the Roar Bank, off Dymchurch, Kent, at 1 a.m. on the morning of 11th March 1860. Roar Bank is a shallow sand ridge running parallel to the shore about a mile off. The *Woodcote* had left the London Docks on the afternoon of 9th March for Adelaide carrying general goods. The weather was squally, with a heavy fall of snow, which, with the haze, was bad enough to obscure the coast lights. The weather was described as 'thick' and there had been a strong set of the flood tide inshore to the Eastward.

Over several days, the cargo had been got off and, with the assistance of the coastguard, the vessel eventually came away and was subsequently towed back to London. There had been no loss of life. An investigation by the Board of Trade, instituted at the Greenwich Police Court, and conducted by Mr. Traill (magistrate) and Cpt. Harris (nautical assessor), determined that although Cpt. Fleming had been generally vigilant in the circumstances, the lead had been 'used too little' given the circumstances of the weather. ('Lead' refers to the cord, knotted at fathom lengths, with a lead-weighted end which was thrown overboard to measure the depth of the sea.)

Following repair the *Woodcote* again set sail for Adelaide with a new cargo, for the original cargo which had been removed in order to bring her off the Roar Bank had been transported to London and auctioned off as sea-damaged. Her cladding was renewed again in 1869 and 1871. From 1874 she disappears from the listings.

SOURCES:
Lloyd's Registers (LR)
Mercantile Naval Lists (MNL)
Lloyd's List (LL)
The South Australian Advertiser (Adelaide, S.A.). Sat. 5th May 1860
The Cornwall Chronicle (Launceston, Tasmania). Wed. 20th June 1860
www.rootschat.com/forum/index.php
www.boards.ancestry.com
www.blaxland.com/ozships/years/arrive/212.htm

Appendix 3 ~ a family tree

This diagram includes, in addition to immediate family members, others referred to in the text, including mourners and pall-bearers at John's Funeral.

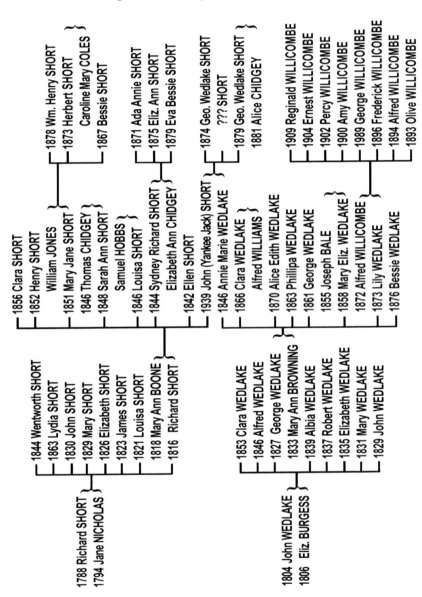

Appendix 4: Voyages of the *Crystal Bell* - Jan 1880-Dec 1882

DATE ARRIVE	PORT	DATE DEPART	DAYS IN PORT	DAYS TO NEXT
1880				
	Charlestown	Jan 13		6
Jan19	Antwerp	Feb 14	26	9
Feb23	Penzance	Mar 3	8	5
Mar 8	London	Mar 21	13	9
Mar 30	Hayle	Apr 7	8	4
Apr 11	Cardiff	Apr 19	8	6
Apr 25	Penzance	May 4	9	4
May 8	Watchet	May 19	11	1
May 20	Cardiff	May 25	5	6
Jun 1	Caen	Jun 15	14	9
Jun 24	Cardiff	Jul 1	7	11
July 16	Charlestown	Jul 13	28	7
July 20	Antwerp	Aug 2	13	
Aug ?	Barr.in Furness	Sep 1		8
Sept 9	Hanley	Sep 30	21	6
Oct 6	Limerick	Oct 23	17	37
Nov 29	Boulogne	Dec 15	16	2
Dec 17	London	Jan 9	25	20
1881				
Jan 29	Liverpool	Mar 2 "Laid up"	3?	1J
Mar 15	Barnstaple	Mar 28	13	14
Apr 11	Cardiff	Apr 23	12	10
May 3	Charlestown	May 17	14	3
May 21	Antwerp	Jun 10	20	11
Jun21	Belfast	July 4	13	4
Jul 8	Newport	Jul 17	9	6
Jul 23	Cork	July 29	6	4
Aug 2	Newport	Aug 9	4	8
Aug 17	Ballinacurra	Aug 30	13	3
Sep 2	Newport	Oct 8	36	16
Oct 24	Cork	Nov 12	19	7

DATE ARRIVE	PORT	DATE DEPART	DAYS IN PORT	DAYS TO NEXT
1881 (cont'd)				
Nov 19	Cardiff	Dec 2	13	8
Dec 10	Dartmouth	Dec 22	12	0
Dec 22	Paington	Dec 30	8	4
Jan 3	Shields			
1882				
Jan 25	Paignton	Feb 3	9	4
Feb 7	Pritton(? Bay)	Feb 15	8	6
Feb 21	Torquay	Mar 3	10	0
Mar 3	Totnes	Mar 3		0
Mar 3	Dartmouth	Mar 4	1	8
Mar 12	Aberdeen	Mar 21	9	4
Mar 25	Shields	Mar 31	6	8
Apr 8	Paignton	Apr 24	16	10
May 4	Shields	May 6	2	8
May 14	Paignton	May 2?		
May 26	Shields	Jun 1	8	15
Jun 16	Paignton	Jun 22	6	0
Jun 22	Totnes	Jul 1	9	4?
Jul 5	Yarmouth	Jul 11	6	2
Jul 13	Shields	July 16	3	15
Jul 31	Paignton	Aug 11	11	6
Aug 17	Shields	Aug 23	6	11
Sep 2	Paignton	Sep 11	9	9
Sep 20	Shields	Sep 28	8	9
Oct 7	Paignton	Oct 14	7	7
Oct 21	Shields	Oct 30	9	9
Nov 13	Dartmouth	Nov 30	17	8
Dec 8	Shields	Dec 21	13	17
1883				
Jan 7	Paignton			

160

Appendix 5: Source of songs/poems quoted in the text

Adieu Sweet Lovely Nancy. Song from the repertoire of the Copper Family of Sussex. Other versions have variously been collected and the theme is ubiquitous in traditional songs.

Billy Riley. One of John Short's shanties.

Blackball Line, The. One of John Short's shanties.

Blow, Boys, Blow. One of John Short's shanties.

Bully Boat, The. One of John Short's rarer shanties.

Carry Him To The Burying Ground. One of John Short's shanties.

Cheerly Man. One of John Short's shanties.

Coffin-ship Owner's Lament, A. Anon. Contemporary broadsheet verse. Published in Jones (2006).

Crossing The Bar. A poem by Alfred Lord Tennyson.

Dead Horse Shanty. Many versions. This one is NOT from John Short.

Donkey Riding. Learnt by Stan Hugill from Spike Sennit, although widespread.

Gallant Frigate Amphitrite, The. a.k.a. *Rounding the Horn*. Collected by Anne Gilchrist from Mr. W. Bolton, Southport, Lancs. May 1907. Several other version collected.

Go To Sea No More. A Liverpool forebitter (leisure-time song) with a chorus borrowed from *Shanghai Brown*.

Home Dearest Home. Several versions exist. This version has been in our repertoire so long we cannot remember where we got it from.

I Wish I Was With Nancy. One of John Short's shanties, a contemporary parody of *I Wish I Was In Dixie*.

Jack Ashore. Also known as *Jack Tar*. Collected by Ralph Vaughan Williams from an un-named singer in Hadleigh Workhouse.

Knock A Man Down. One of John Short's shanties. An early form of the shanty better known as *Blow The Man Down*.

Leave Her Johnny, Leave Her. One of John Short's shanties.

Limejuice Ship,The. A forebitter that was occasionally used as a pumping shanty. This version from John Buckingham of Padstow.

Lowlands (Dollar and a Half). One of John Short's shanties.

Old Stormey. One of John Short's shanties.

Outward Bound. Also known as *Outward and Homeward Bound*. Widespread forebitter with many variants, usually localised to the singer.

Ratcliffe Highway. Another forebitter. Published by William Doeflinger – from Captain Tayleur.

Rio Grand. One of John Short's shanties.

Roll Alabama Roll. Shanty with a true story! The tune and structure borrowed from the African-American songs *Roll the Cotton* and *Roll the Woodpile Down*.

Roll, Bullies, Roll. Also known as *Liverpool Judies.* Very widespread.

Round The Corner Sally. One of John Short's shanties.

Sailor's Life, A. Folk Song Journal 1 99. There are many versions, but this one comes from Henry Hills of Lodsworth, Sussex.

Sailors Way, The. Capstan & pumping shanty, published by Hugill and Doeflinger.

Seraphina. Learnt by Stan Hugill from Irish sailor Jack Connolly. Published in Hugill (1960).

Shanadar. One of John Short's shanties.

Sing Fare You Well. One of John Short's shanties.

Stormalong. One of John Short's shanties.

Stowing Sugar In The Hold. Originates probably as a Mississippi riverboarman's chant. Popularised by William Pint & Felicia Dale who had it from Marc Bridgham who probably made it into the song as currently known.

Swansea Town. Collected by Frank Gardiner, from William Randall, Harsley, Hants. June 1908. Other versions appear as *Adieu Sweet Lovely Nancy* and *The Holy Ground.*

Sweet Nightingale. John Short's non-shanty song.

Watchet Sailor, The. Collected by Cecil Sharp from Cpt.Lewis at Minehead, Somerset, on 10th January1906.

Won't You Go My Way. One of John Short's shanties.

Bibliography and References

Books, magazine articles, and authors quoted, drawn on or referred to:

- *ch.9, Braunton Vessels* in Robert D'Arcy Andrew et al. (2007) *Braunton: Home of the last Sailing Coasters.* (Braunton & District Museum, Braunton, Devon)
- *Clergy List.* (1912 onward) Kelly Directories. London
- *Crockford's Clerical Directory* (1929 onwards) Oxford University Press
- Lloyd's Registers (held @ National Maritime Museum, Cornwall)
- Merchantile Navy Lists (held @ National Maritime Museum, Cornwall)

Abel, E. Lawrence. (2000) *Singing the New Nation – How Music Shaped the Confederacy 1861-1865.* (Stackpole Books, Mechanicsburg, Pennsylvania)

Bailey, Hiram. (1925) *Shanghied Out of 'Frisco in the 'Nineties.* (Heath Cranton, London)

Bouquet, M.R. (1958) *The Old Shantyman.* Country Life Annual

Bouquet, M.R. (1959) *No Gallant Ship.* (Hollis & Carte, London)

Bouquet, M.R. (1971) *Master and Men* (David & Charles, Newton Abbot)

Chapman, Cpt. Charles. (1868) *All About Ships.* (Colyer, London). Facsimile reproduction: print-on-demand, 2010

Clayton, Lawrence A. (1980) *Chinese Indentured Labour in Peru.* History Today v.30 issue 6

Cutler, Carl C. (1984) *Greyhounds of the Sea* (Patrick Stephens Ltd., Wellingborough) (First published 1930)

Doerflinger, W. M. (1990) *Songs of the Sailor and Lumberman* (Meyerbooks, Glenwood, Illinois) (first published as *Shantymen & Shantyboys.* The Macmillan Company, New York. 1951)

Draper, Nick (2007) *'Possessing Slaves': Ownership, Compemsation and Metropolitan Society in Britain at the time of Emancipation 1834-40* in History Workshop Journal, vol.64, issue 1, pp74-102

Harlow, Frederick Pease (2004) *Chanteying Aboard American Ships.* (Mystic Seaport Museum Inc., Mystic, CT.) (first published by Barre Pub. Co. Inc., 1962)

Hugill, Stan. (1960) *Shanties From the Seven Seas.* (Routledge and Kegan Paul. London)

Hugill, Stan (1967) *Sailortown.* (Routledge and Kegan Paul. London)

Hugill, Stan. (2006) *The Bosun's Locker.* (David Heron Publishing, Todmorton, Yorks) (Collected articles from Spin magazine 1962-1973)

Hurley, Jack. (n/k) *Town Crier with the Golden Voice.* (photocopy from Bouquet notebooks)

James, Tony. (2003) *Yankee Jack: Chantey Man.* Traditional Boats & Tall Ships (Feb/March 2003)

James, Tony. (2003) *Listening to Yankee Jack*. The Exmoor Magazine no. 25
James, Tony. (2006) *Yankee Jack Sails Again*. (Seafarer Books, Rendlesham, Suffolk)
Jones, Nicolette. (2006) *The Plimsoll Sensation*. (Little Brown. London)
Karpeles. Maud. (1967*) Cecil Sharp. His Life and Work.* (Routledge & Kegan Paul, London)
Mayhew, Henry. (1950) *London's Underworld*. (Bracken Books, London). (edited edition of Mayhew's *London Labour and The London Poor* published 1851-1862)
Norman, Ben. (1987) *Yankee Jack*. Exmoor Review 1987
Norman, Ben. (2002) *Tales of Watchet Harbour*. (Privately published: 1st edition 1985, 3rd edition, revised, 2002)
Olinger, John Peter. (2011*) The Guano Age in Peru*. in History Today, vol.30 issue 6. (http://www.historytoday.com/john-peter-olinger/guano-age-peru)
Patten, Jacqueline (2011) *Yankee Jack*. in What's Afoot: Devon's Folk Magazine vol.97
Plimsoll, Samuel (1873) *Our Seamen; An Appeal* (Virtue Co., London) (reproduced using OCR scanning by General Books, 2009)
Pope, Peter E. (2004) *Fish into Wine. The Newfoundland Plantation in the Seventeenth Century*. (The University of North Carolina Press)
Rouse, Andrew C. (1989) *Tales From Watchet*. (English Learner's Library, Budapest)
Sechrest, Prof. Larry J. (2007) *American Shipbuilders in the Heyday of Sail: Entrepreneurs and the State* (Libertarian Alliance, London)
Sharp, Cecil J. (1914) *English Folk-Chanteys* (Simpkin Marshall Ltd., Schott & Co. Ltd., London)
Stainer, Peter H. *The copper ore trade of South West England in the Nineteenth century*. Journal of Transport History. (http://www.aditnow.co.uk/documents/personal-album-272/Copper.pdf)
Strangeways, A. H. Fox. (1933) *Cecil Sharp*. (*O.U.P.*)
Terry, R. R. (1924) *The Shanty Book Part II*. (J. Curwen & Sons Ltd., London) (Part 1 [1921] has none of Short's versions)

Internet sources:

wapedia.mobi/en/High_Sheriff_of_Berkshire
www.crewlist.org.uk/crewlist.html
www.irishshipwrecks.com
www.mauritius.org.uk/History.htm
www.quantockonline.co.uk/news/2008/yankee_jack.html
www.swanseamariners.org.uk

www.theshipslist.com/ships/australia/SAassistedindex.htm
www.umbermusic.co.uk/sssnotes.htm
www.pro.rcip-chin.gc.ca/bd-dl/nav-ship-eng.jsp
www.victorianweb.org/index.html
www1.somerset.gov.uk/archives/Exmoor/normanbsummary1.htm
  and sources quoted for individual ships as given in appendix 2

Newspaper and mss. sources:

Bridgwater Port Shipping Register 1786-1906. (Somerset Heritage Centre)
Cecil Sharp's field notebooks April – September 1914 (Vaughan Williams
    Memorial Library)
Cecil Sharp's mss. nos. 2877 – 3059 (Vaughan Williams Memorial Library)
Census returns ~ 1841-1911 (via www.findmypast.co.uk)
Cornwall Chronicle (Launceston, Tasmania). Wednesday 20th June 1860
Crew Lists ~ Bridgwater registered boats (Somerset Heritage Centre)
         ~ *Conference,* with log books (Bristol Records Office)
         ~ various, some with log books (Maritime Archive, Uni. of
            Newfoundland)
Grahame E Farr mss. ~ notes on Bristol registered ships 1836-1850 & 1851-1899
    (Bristol Records Office)
Index to Lloyd's List (microfilm copies held @ Guildhall Library, London)
Lloyd's List (microfilm copies held @ Guildhall Library, London)
London Patents Office: (Muntz yellow metal)
patents   1832, October 22 - N° 6325,
           1832, December 17 - N° 6347
           1846, October 15 - N° 11,410
Michael Bouquet's notebooks (copies provided by Mark Myers)
Ships Registry Archive ~ Liverpool Maritime Museum
Somerset County Gazette 15th April 1933
Somerset County Gazette. 22nd April 1933
Somerset County Gazette. 19th July 1974 - 'Peter Hesp's Notebook' (regular
    feature): *A Solo Part for Yankee Jack*
South Australian Advertiser (Adelaide, S.A.). Saturday 5th May 1860
The Times. Wednesday 12th April 1933
Watchet Hobblers Assoc. account and minute books (Somerset Heritage Centre)
Watchet Shipowners 1865-97 (Somerset Heritage Centre)
West Somerset Free Press. Saturday August 29th 1931
West Somerset Free Press. Saturday April 15th 1933
West Somerset Free Press. Saturday 22nd April 1933